home
with ben

at home with ben

with

great family food for every occasion

Ben O'Donoghue

hardie grant books

MELBOURNE · LONDON

To Rose Gray

You had faith in me and inspired me and evoked passion in everyone. You will be missed and always remembered.

contents

Cooking, eating and sharing
the experience of food is such
a beautiful thing.

intr

Throughout my life, food has always been a source of pleasure. From the time I spent helping and watching my grandmother make cakes, both in the UK and here in Australia, to my early youth and Tom Sawyer–like adventures of fishing, camping and cooking outdoors in the north-west of Australia, followed by my professional discoveries through travels in Europe and Asia, cooking and eating has never failed to excite and inspire me.

I've always been overwhelmed by the sheer vastness of the world of food – the information, recipes, techniques and cultural diversity. When I was a young apprentice I felt inadequate and hopelessly naive. I thought I could never possibly know it all, or remember everything I had learnt so far or would learn in the future. Thankfully, this is still true. It is this feeling of discovery that drives me and most chefs onwards in the search for new and wonderful flavours, and it is these discoveries that are our reward.

The greatest reward, though, is the ability to share these discoveries and experiences with the people you love. Food brings people together; it breaks down barriers, and communicates across language and culture. It is the greatest diplomat, romantic and seductress.

My first standalone book, *Outdoor*, embraced this concept across the global world of the barbecue. With this book, I wanted to share a snapshot of my life in food so far. The sheer enormity of this task was overwhelming – how could I decide which recipes to include from a professional career of twenty-three years of cooking and eating?

Stepping back and looking at things objectively, I decided to focus on the recipes that represent the concept of shared experience. Dishes that have brought me pleasure and whose memory I treasure. The dishes that have been cooked for me by friends, my favourites from the many I have cooked in restaurants I have run or worked in, the ones I have eaten at other restaurants, those I have cooked in various cooking shows that have not yet been published, and also the dishes I cook in my current restaurant in Brisbane, the South Bank Surf Club.

at home with ben

I also wanted to look at different occasions in which to share these experiences and recipes. Since I have moved back to Australia from the UK, my life has changed incredibly and become more rich in terms of lifestyle. The ability to entertain in more space and in better weather drives us outside into our backyards or decks, bringing the outside in! We tend to do breakfast and brunch more often. We eat lighter and also eat more Asian-influenced dishes, as the freshness, spiciness and availability of produce is suited to those cuisines.

Importantly, eating well costs money! As a father of three, I wanted to share recipes that are everyday and family-oriented, while also practising something we seem to have forgotten or do little about these days – home economics! Making use of leftovers is something previous generations lived with, especially after the war and into the 1950s and '60s.

We need to move away from our disposable culture. By cooking larger cuts of meat and poultry, we can use the leftovers to create dishes over the next two or three days. For example, cook up a lovely roast beef, chicken or pork on the Sunday, and then use the leftovers in a rice dish the next night, and make stocks and soups with the meat bones.

I also encourage you to spend a little more on produce that is free range, rare breed, organic or slow. It is better in terms of animal husbandry and welfare, while also being less intensively grown. It means you throw less away, which in turn reduces what goes into landfill. If we are to enjoy this world we live in, we need to respect and use its fruits well.

I hope these recipes bring you pleasure when cooking, eating and sharing food!

love Ben

breakfast, lunch & in between

Bloody Mary!

I first made these in the UK on the TV show *Saturday Kitchen* with my mate Curtis Stone as part of an Aussie Hangover Cure segment – it was Australia Day. That segment got Curtis and me the job doing *Surfing the Menu*, so this recipe has a special place in my heart. Serves 4–6

220 ml bottle HP Sauce
60 ml bottle Tabasco sauce
2 litres tomato juice
juice of 4 limes
2 tablespoons celery salt (see recipe
   below)
1 head celery
ice
vodka (optional)

Combine the HP Sauce, Tabasco, tomato juice, lime juice and celery salt in a large bowl and whisk together. Check the seasoning and add more tomato juice if needed. I like my bloody Mary quite seasoned and spicy.

Trim and wash several celery sticks to use as stirrers. Fill two jugs with ice and pour over the virgin Mary mix. Add the celery stick stirrers to the jug. If required, add vodka to desired strength.

Celery salt

Celery salt is a great way to use up all those dark green celery leaves that most people throw away, and adds wonderful flavour to fish, poultry and grilled meats. When making any flavoured salt, it's imperative that you start with a top-quality salt. I always use coarse rock salt. Makes 165 g

2 cups dark celery leaves
¾ cup coarse rock salt
1 teaspoon celery seeds (optional)
¼ teaspoon cumin seeds (optional)

Wash the celery leaves then spin dry or allow them to drain well. Place the leaves in a large mortar, along with ½ cup of salt. Use a grinding motion to make a paste, which may be quite wet at first.

Add up to ¼ cup of salt and grind until the paste is just moist and the leaves are well ground into the salt; you may not need to add the full ¼ cup of salt. The salt should be a nice pale to medium green colour, depending on the darkness of the celery leaves.

Preheat the oven to 100°C.

Line a baking tray with baking paper. Combine the salt with the celery and cumin seeds (if using), then spread the mixture evenly over the paper. Place in the oven for around 1 hour, or until completely dry.

The salt will keep for 1 month if stored in an airtight container or re-usable grinder.

Basic muffins

Muffins are pretty commonplace these days – you can't pass a café or high street coffee joint without seeing them. They are the perfect breakfast on the go! These ones are dead easy to make, so keep a little extra money in your pocket and make your own.

   If you want to add fruit or chocolate to this basic muffin recipe, go right ahead. For banana muffins, just add a couple of mashed ripe bananas to the egg, milk and oil mixture. If you want to add fruit like diced apple or pear, combine it with the dry ingredients. Half a cup of chopped chocolate is great with the banana!

   When I'm cooking muffins, I find non-stick muffin moulds are best – you can line them with baking paper for presentation if you like. Makes 12

225 g plain flour
100 g caster sugar
2 teaspoons baking powder
½ teaspoon salt
1 egg
1 cup milk
120 ml sunflower oil

Preheat the oven to 200°C.

Combine the flour, caster sugar and baking powder in a large bowl and make a well in the centre. Place the remaining ingredients in a jug and combine, then pour into the centre of the well. Mix until just combined (don't overmix).

Spoon the mixture into standard size muffin moulds. Place in the oven to bake for about 20 minutes, or until the muffins are well risen and springy to the touch.

Fruity loaf

My mate Jamie Oliver makes great bread – it must be because of all those lessons from Gennaro! This recipe is a nod to Jamie's recipe, though I prefer slightly different fruit in my loaf. The addition of seeds and nuts is always a good option, especially flax and sunflower seeds. Makes 1 loaf

1 cup currants
1 cup raisins
1 cup dried figs
1 teaspoon ground cinnamon
pinch of ground cloves
800 g strong bread flour, plus extra for dusting
200 g wholemeal flour
2 tablespoons salt
2 × 7 g sachets dried yeast
2 tablespoons dark golden syrup
butter, to serve, plus extra for buttering

Place the dried fruit, cinnamon and cloves in a blender and pulse three or four times to chop.

Sift the flours and salt into a large bowl. Combine the yeast and golden syrup with 600 ml of warm water. Make a well in the centre of the flour and work in about half the yeast and water mixture, gradually bringing in the flour from the edges. When combined, add the remaining yeast and water mixture, along with the dried fruit, and incorporate into a dough. If the dough is dry, add a little more water until it's soft but not sticky.

Knead the dough in the bowl or on a lightly floured surface by rolling, pushing and folding it over for about 8 minutes.

Lightly flour the dough and knead it into an even, round shape. Place the dough in the mixing bowl, cover with a damp cloth and leave it to prove in a draught-free, warmish spot. It may take an hour – the more slowly it proves, the better the flavour.

Preheat the oven to 180°C.

Once the dough has risen, punch it back to knock the air out of it. Butter and flour a 26 cm loaf tin and shape the dough to fit into it. Leave it to prove for another hour, until the dough has doubled in size. It should rise above the top of the tin.

When ready to cook, carefully place the loaf tin in the oven and bake for 45 minutes. Remove the loaf from the tin and bake for a further 10 minutes.

Leave the fruit loaf to cool on a wire rack, then serve with butter. It's also lovely toasted.

Corn and coriander hotcakes

Since Bill Granger made hotcakes über trendy by serving them at his eponymous cafés in Sydney, they've become a breakfast staple.

I cooked these hotcakes for a UK dance outfit, the Friendly Fires, at the Splendour in the Grass music festival in Byron Bay. I served them topped with Aussie Asian Eggs (page 36), but they're equally good alongside avocado and bacon with chilli or tomato salsa and fried eggs. To cook them, you can use a non-stick blini pan, large flat griddle pan or barbecue plate. Serves 4

1½ cups plain flour, sifted

1 teaspoon baking powder

1 teaspoon salt

4 eggs, separated

¾ cup milk

1 cup ricotta

1 cup canned corn kernels, drained

bunch of coriander, leaves chopped

salt

freshly ground black pepper

50 g butter

Combine the flour, baking powder and salt in a large bowl. Make a well in the centre and add the egg yolks and milk. Whisk until smooth.

Loosely fold in the ricotta, corn and chopped coriander leaves. Season with salt and pepper.

Whisk the egg whites until they form soft peaks, then gently fold into the batter.

Melt a teaspoon of butter in a frying pan over medium heat. Drop in tablespoons of batter to form 6–8 cm round hotcakes, making sure that the mix is evenly distributed. Cook for 3–4 minutes, until lightly golden. Use a palette knife to turn over and continue to cook for another 2–3 minutes.

Cook the hotcakes in batches, keeping them warm under a tea towel or in the oven.

Fruit salad

Fruit is a great way to start the day, and also the perfect way to finish a meal. What's hard about a fruit salad? Well, nothing really, but the difference between a good fruit salad and a wonderful one is the ripeness of the fruit and the way it's put together. This is where the lime and mint sugar come in, lifting the flavour and adding another dimension.

The fruit I've listed below is just a suggestion. For a dramatic effect, try using dragon fruit or star fruit. Rather than cutting the fruit into cubes, use their interesting natural shapes to accentuate the presentation of the dish. Leaving the red skin intact on dragon fruit contrasts brilliantly with the white flesh and small black seeds. Serves 4

¼ ripe pineapple
2 mangoes (Kingston pride or Bowen varieties are best)
¼ ripe red pawpaw
2 navel oranges, segmented
2 ripe bananas
2 passionfruit
6 kiwi berries or 2 kiwi fruit
strawberries
juice of 1 lime

Mint and lime sugar
2 tablespoons caster sugar
4 mint leaves
finely grated zest of 1 lime

Use the natural shape of the fruit to determine how you will cut each one – into thin slices, long crescent fingers, cross-sections and segments.

Arrange the fruit on a large platter or in a bowl and squeeze over the lime juice.

To make the mint and lime sugar, pound the caster sugar and mint leaves in a mortar with a pestle until the sugar is moist but not wet. It should be green and have a minty flavour and aroma. Add the lime zest.

Sprinkle the mint and lime sugar over the fruit salad and serve.

Brioche

Brioche is a French staple, associated with foie gras terrine and Marie Antoinette, who said in relation to the starving poor of Paris: 'Let them eat brioche.'

It's one of those breads that can be transformed from a fairly humble egg and butter dough to form the basis of glorious French toast, a bread and butter pudding, a great burger bun or the most divine breadcrumbs for fish. Makes 1 loaf or 6–8 buns

275 g soft butter, plus extra for buttering
550 g plain flour, plus extra for dusting
60 g caster sugar
30 g fresh yeast or 7 g sachet dried yeast
90 ml tepid milk
7 eggs
1 tablespoon sesame seeds

Butter and flour a 26 cm loaf tin or a baking tray if you are making buns.

Combine the flour and caster sugar in a mixing machine.

Dissolve the yeast in the tepid milk, then add to the flour mixture along with 6 eggs. Mix for about 15 minutes, or until very smooth and elastic. Add the butter and mix until it's totally incorporated into the dough. Cover with a damp cloth and allow to prove until doubled in size.

Preheat the oven to 180°C.

Knock back the dough, then using wet hands roll it into three balls. Place in the prepared loaf tin, and leave to prove again until the balls of dough have doubled in size.

If you are making buns, divide the knocked back dough into 6–8 balls using wet hands. Stretch and tuck the dough back under itself to create smooth, round buns. Place the buns on the prepared baking tray, making sure you leave enough room in between each bun to allow them to prove until they have doubled in size.

Lightly beat the remaining egg to make an egg wash. Gently coat the dough with the egg wash, then bake for 30 minutes for a loaf, or 20 minutes for buns.

Remove from the oven and allow to cool before using.

Brioche is a French staple, associated with foie gras terrine and Marie Antoinette, who said in relation to the starving poor of Paris:

'Let them eat brioche.'

Eggy bread with poached peaches

This recipe is great for using up leftover stale pastries like croissants or brioche. Its proper name is French toast but I like the more homely name eggy bread. Serves 2

2 eggs
2 tablespoons milk
1 teaspoon lemon thyme
2 teaspoons caster sugar
1 large croissant, sliced in half horizontally
50 g butter
poached stone fruit (see recipe below)
icing sugar, to serve
thickened cream, to serve
sprigs of mint, to serve

Combine the eggs, milk, thyme and caster sugar in a large bowl and whisk well.

Place the croissant slices in the egg mixture for about 2 minutes each side, allowing them to soak up as much liquid as possible.

Gently melt the butter in a large frying pan or on the grill plate of your barbecue, until foaming. Place the well-soaked croissant slices cut-side down on the cooking surface and cook for about 2 minutes, or until golden. Use an eggflip to turn the eggy bread and gently cook for a further 2 minutes.

When cooked, remove to a serving dish and top with poached fruit. Dust with icing sugar and serve with cream and mint sprigs.

Poached stone fruit

It's great to poach your own fruit for this recipe. Poached fruit will keep for a week in the refrigerator. To extend the shelf life to several months, store the fruit in a sterilised jar. Simple place the empty jar, with the lid closed, in a saucepan of water. Bring to the boil and simmer for 10 minutes, then allow the jar to cool with the lid still closed.

500 g golden caster sugar
1 litre mineral water
zest and juice of 1 lemon
zest and juice of 1 orange
1½ tablespoons cognac
1 vanilla pod
1 cinnamon stick
1 star anise
6 ripe peaches or nectarines,
   or 10 apricots

Place all the ingredients except the fruit in a saucepan and bring to the boil. Simmer for 10 minutes. Remove from the heat and add the fruit. Place a small plate on top of the fruit to keep it submerged. Allow the fruit and liquid to cool completely.

When cool, transfer the poached fruit to a clean airtight container and store in the fridge until required. To serve, peel the fruit, cut in half along the natural groove and remove the seed.

Homemade crumpets

When I was a kid and my mum bought crumpets, they never seemed to last more than five minutes in our house. I remember eating them with so much honey and butter it would pool on the plate, and once the crumpets were devoured the plate would be licked clean!

A few tips when cooking these. First, you'll need crumpet rings or deep egg rings. The batter should be the consistency of pouring cream; if it's too thick it won't develop the holes that make crumpets what they are, and if it's too thin the batter will run outside the crumpet ring. The right heat is also important – if it's too hot, the crumpet will burn before it rises. You can cook these on the barbecue or stovetop, but always start with a test run first. Leftover crumpets (if there are any!) can be toasted the next day. Makes 8 crumpets

300 g plain flour

1 teaspoon caster sugar

7 g sachet dried yeast

175 ml milk, room temperature

175 ml soda water, room temperature

½ teaspoon bicarbonate of soda

1 teaspoon salt

vegetable oil or non-stick cooking spray

butter, honey or jam, to serve

Sift the flour, caster sugar and yeast into a large bowl. Stir in the milk, then add the soda water and whisk until smooth.

Cover the bowl with plastic wrap and allow to rest for about 1½ hours, or until doubled in volume.

Beat in the bicarb and salt. Heat a heavy-bottomed frying pan or the griddle plate on your barbecue until medium–hot. Oil or spray the inside of the crumpet rings, as well as the pan or barbecue plate. Place the rings on the cooking surface, making sure they are evenly flat.

Spoon 3–3½ tablespoons of batter into each ring and gently cook for 6–7 minutes, or until the batter is set and covered with little holes. Turn the crumpets over and cook for another 2 minutes. The bottom should be golden brown and the top only slightly coloured.

Remove the rings and serve the crumpets straight away with lashings of butter, honey or your favourite jam.

Omelettes for beginners

An omelette is a classic breakfast or brunch egg dish, and the perfect test of a cook's skill. It's something you might want to make for that special someone – the occasion is up to you!

This recipe is for a single serve, as perfect omelettes need to be cooked one at a time. You'll need a non-stick 24-centimetre omelette pan. If you want to add a filling – for example, mushrooms – it's best to prepare it separately beforehand and keep it warm until you're ready to serve.

I love the traditional addition of fine herbs, added to the egg mix prior to cooking. Try a teaspoon each of chopped chives, chervil and tarragon. To garnish, slices of smoked salmon and some sour cream and chives would be perfect. Serves 1

3 eggs
salt
freshly ground black pepper
50 g butter, plus extra to serve

Break the eggs into a bowl and whisk them together with a fork. Season with salt and pepper.

Heat the omelette pan over medium heat. When hot, add the butter and heat until it melts and gently foams. Add the beaten eggs. Gently move the egg mixture around the pan occasionally – the idea is not to scramble the eggs, but to move them around in the first few moments before allowing them to set. You don't want to allow the eggs to cook for too long or at too high a temperature.

The omelette is ready to serve when the bottom is set and lightly golden, and the top is just runny, or what chefs call baveuse.

Shaking the pan to loosen it a little, slide the omelette towards the edge of the pan. Use a palette knife to flip the omelette over by a third.

Bring your serving plate up to the side of the pan and slide the folded edge of the omelette onto the plate. Fold the remaining edge over to create a cigar or torpedo shape.

To serve, brush a little extra butter over the omelette. If you're adding a filling, make an incision down the middle of the omelette and spoon it in.

Spanish tortilla

½ cup olive oil
3 onions, sliced
1 garlic clove, chopped
4 waxy potatoes, par-boiled, peeled and diced
6 eggs
salt
freshly ground black pepper

Preheat the oven to 180°C.

Heat 2 tablespoons of olive oil in a frying pan over medium heat. Add the onion and garlic and slowly fry for 10 minutes, until golden and soft. Remove from the pan and set aside.

Heat 2 tablespoons of olive oil in the frying pan. When hot, fry the potatoes until golden and crispy. Drain and combine with the onions.

Whisk the eggs, then mix them into the onion and potato mixture. Season with salt and pepper.

Heat the remaining olive oil in a 25 cm non-stick ovenproof frying pan over medium heat. When hot, pour in the tortilla mixture. Place the pan in the preheated oven and cook the tortilla for 10–15 minutes, or until firm.

Remove from the oven and turn out onto a plate. Allow the tortilla to cool before serving.

Mixed berry and ricotta crepes

Crepes are a childhood favourite of mine. My daughter Ruby loves them for breakfast, simply topped with some honey, but it's great to make something a little bit special from time to time. Frozen mixed berries are an inexpensive and fantastic way to tart up the humble crepe.

Serves 4

1 cup plain flour
pinch of salt
4 eggs
2 cups milk
40 g butter
crème fraîche, to serve
sprigs of mint, to serve
icing sugar, sifted, to serve

Ricotta filling
250 g smooth ricotta
finely grated zest of 1 lemon
honey, to taste

Berry sauce
2 cups frozen mixed berries
1 cup icing sugar

To make the crepe batter, sift the flour and salt into a large bowl. Whisk the eggs and milk together in a separate bowl. Make a well in the centre of the flour and slowly add the milk and egg mixture, whisking continuously to bring the flour and liquid together to form a smooth pouring cream consistency. Set aside to rest for an hour or so (this can also be done the night before).

Combine the ricotta filling ingredients. The amount of honey you use is up to you; I like it just sweet. Set aside.

Place the mixed berries and icing sugar in a small saucepan and bring to the boil. Simmer for 5 minutes, then allow to cool.

Gently heat a non-stick frying pan or crepe pan. Using a brush or some paper towel, lightly butter the surface of the pan. Add 3 tablespoons crepe batter to the pan, quickly swirling it around to ensure a thin, even coating of batter. Ideally, the crepe should be thin enough to see your hand through when you hold it up.

Cook the crepe on one side for 2–3 minutes, then, using a palette knife, turn it over and cook for a further 1–2 minutes. Transfer to a plate. Cook the crepes in batches, making two crepes per serve and keeping them warm under a folded tea towel.

To serve, place a spoonful of the ricotta mixture in the middle of each crepe and spread it around a little. Fold the crepes in half, then in half again and place them on serving plates. Spoon the berries and sauce over the top and finish with a dollop of crème fraîche, a sprig of mint and a dusting of icing sugar.

Rice porridge with fish

I love this porridge for breakfast. It takes my mind straight to Thailand, and the buffet breakfasts they serve at beach resort hotels in Phuket. For most Westerners, the idea of porridge with fish would be most surreal. I think it's so nourishing and flavoursome, I would bypass the bacon and eggs any day for this breakfast.

It's not so hard to make this at home, especially if you're used to making up chicken stock with leftover bones. You can buy the crispy fried onions and garlic from Asian food stores. Serves 4

1 litre chicken stock (see page 190)
175 g rice polenta
400 g white fish fillets (whiting is best)
8 scallops (optional)
2 spring onions, finely sliced
1 cup crispy fried onions
1 tablespoon crispy fried garlic
2 tablespoons chopped chives, to garnish
4 small green chillies, finely chopped,
    to serve
⅓ cup fish sauce, to serve

Pour the chicken stock into a saucepan and bring to the boil. Whisk in the polenta, and keep whisking until the mixture is thick like porridge. Leave to simmer for 5 minutes.

Turn the heat down to a gentle simmer, add the fish fillets and gently poach. When just done, add the scallops (if using). Mix the porridge to break up the fish evenly.

Just before serving, add the spring onions. Divide the porridge between four bowls, top with the fried onions and garlic, and garnish with a sprinkling of chives.

Combine the chilli and fish sauce, and serve with the porridge as a seasoning.

Bruschetta with tomato

This recipe comes from my early-morning starts at the River Café in London. As there would usually be some bruschetta left over from the night before, the first piece of equipment to be turned on each morning was the chargrill to cook the morning shift's breakfast.

One of the toppings that I particularly liked was anchovies, olive oil and freshly picked marjoram. It was probably due to salt cravings from the well-lubricated evening before, but I still love these savoury starts to the day. Ideally the tomatoes should be green zebra or tigerella, though vine-ripened or truss tomatoes will suffice. Serves 4

4 large slices sourdough bread
1 garlic clove
⅓ cup extra-virgin olive oil
4 tablespoons ricotta
salt
freshly ground black pepper
2 large heirloom tomatoes, room
   temperature, sliced
8 anchovy fillets
1 tablespoon roughly chopped marjoram

Using either a griddle pan or barbecue, grill the slices of sourdough until nicely toasted. Remove from the grill and immediately rub one side of the bread once or twice with the garlic clove. Drizzle with the olive oil.

Season the ricotta with salt and pepper. Spread a tablespoon of ricotta across each piece of bruschetta, then add slices of tomato and 2 anchovy fillets.

Top with a sprinkling of marjoram, another drizzle of extra-virgin olive oil and some more pepper.

Aussie Asian eggs

I serve this Aussie breakfast at the South Bank Surf Club in Brisbane – I think it represents the true multicultural nature of Australian food.

It's a great one to cook outside on the barbecue, especially if you are making up a batch of Corn and Coriander Hotcakes (page 20) as well. You will need a side burner on your barbecue, or alternatively you can fry the eggs on the barbecue plate. Note that you can use the deep-frying oil more than once by allowing it to cool after cooking, then straining. Serves 4

1 litre sunflower oil, for deep-frying
8 rashers smoked bacon, rind removed
8 raw king prawn tails, peeled and
    deveined
8 eggs
1 red chilli, chopped, to garnish
2 spring onions, finely sliced, to garnish
oyster sauce, to serve

Pour the oil into a wok and heat to 160°C.

While the oil is heating, grill the bacon for about 5 minutes, or until crispy. Add the prawns and cook for around 3 minutes. Once the bacon and prawns are cooked, keep them warm on the edge of the barbecue.

When the oil is ready, crack the eggs into a cup, then add them to the hot oil, one at a time. Be careful, as the oil will splatter. Cook no more than 2 eggs at a time and push the oil around so they cook evenly. After about 1 minute remove the eggs from the oil and quickly drain them.

To serve, arrange the prawns and bacon on a plate. Top with the deep-fried eggs, garnish with chopped chilli and spring onions and drizzle with oyster sauce.

Potato pancakes with smoked salmon

This recipe is a blend of two that I've used over the years. I used to make one version at Monte's in London, served with seared foie gras – a great combination, though the recipe was a little labour intensive. The other version comes from my mate Darren Simpson on *The Best in Australia*, which involves blending the potatoes with the remaining ingredients while they are hot. It's a far easier way to make the batter and it keeps for a few days.

To cook the pancakes, I use tarte tatin moulds or blini pans. The addition of a poached egg is an optional extra, and to enhance the batter you could add other chopped herbs or corn kernels. Serves 4

500 g waxy potatoes, peeled
3 eggs
3 egg whites
75 ml crème fraîche
4 tablespoons plain flour
½ teaspoon salt
pinch of white pepper
1 tablespoon chopped chives
100 g butter
12 slices smoked salmon, to serve
8 poached eggs (optional), to serve
flat-leaf parsley leaves, to serve
juice of 1 lemon, to serve

Boil the potatoes in salted water. When cooked, drain and allow to steam dry. Place the potatoes in a food processor while still hot, along with the eggs, egg whites, crème fraîche, flour, salt and pepper. Process until smooth. Reserve and allow to cool.

Preheat the oven to 200°C.

When the mixture is cool, add 1 tablespoon chopped chives and combine thoroughly.

Spread 25 g butter in each of the four moulds or blini pans and place in the hot oven. When the butter begins to foam, remove from the oven. Divide the batter between the moulds or pans, return them to the oven and cook for 10 minutes, or until firm and golden on top.

To turn out, place a similar-sized tray or plate over each mould or pan and flip. Using a palette knife or eggflip, turn the pancake over and place in the centre of a serving plate.

Serve the pancakes with slices of smoked salmon, a poached egg (if desired), some parsley leaves and a squeeze of lemon juice.

Tuna salad toastie

This is a perfect summer brunch dish. The crunchy texture of the radish and onion, and the juicy acidity of the beefsteak tomato make this a taste experience. If you're reducing your carbs, replace the bread with cannellini or butter beans, or even chickpeas. A habanero chilli would add a load of spice and flavour to the salad as well. Serves 4

250 g can tuna
1 red onion, finely sliced
4 radishes (I like the French breakfast variety), finely sliced
1 large ripe beefsteak tomato, diced
2 tablespoons chopped flat-leaf parsley leaves
1 tablespoon Japanese mayonnaise
lemon juice
salt
freshly ground black pepper
2 squares of Turkish bread, sliced in half horizontally
1 ripe avocado

Combine the tuna, red onion, radishes, tomato and parsley in a large bowl. Dress with the mayonnaise, add a squeeze of lemon juice and season with salt and pepper.

Toast the Turkish bread – cooking it on the barbecue grill will give it a lovely smoky flavour. Spread the toasted bread with avocado, then top with the salad mixture. Serve with a chilled glass of SSB (semillon sauvignon blanc).

Goat's cheese and spring onion quiche

Who said real men don't eat quiche? It makes a great summer lunch, served with a simple salad and your favourite relish. Serves 4

Pastry

500 g strong flour, plus extra for dusting
1 teaspoon sugar
1½ teaspoons salt
375 g butter
½ teaspoon white wine vinegar
1 egg yolk
100 ml milk

Filling

2 tablespoons olive oil
1 leek, peeled, washed and chopped
3 bunches spring onions, peeled, washed and chopped
1 garlic clove, finely chopped
salt
freshly ground black pepper
150 ml thickened cream
285 g crème fraîche
6 eggs
2 tablespoons grated parmesan
1 tablespoon chopped tarragon
240 g soft goat's cheese

To make the pastry, combine the flour, sugar and salt in a large bowl. Rub in the butter until the mixture is the texture of coarse breadcrumbs. Add the vinegar, egg yolk and milk and combine. Wrap in plastic wrap and refrigerate for at least 1 hour until firm.

To make the spring onion filling, heat the olive oil in a saucepan over medium heat and cook the leek and spring onions for about 10 minutes, until soft but not coloured. Add the garlic and season with salt and pepper. Leave to cool.

Preheat the oven to 180°C. Combine the cream and crème fraîche. Beat in the eggs and add the parmesan. Season to taste.

On a well-floured sheet of baking paper, roll out the pastry to about 1 cm thick. It needs to be large enough to line a 25 x 7 cm deep springform cake tin. Lay the pastry over the tin and gently work it in. Don't worry about the extra bits hanging over the edge; they'll drop off while cooking and keep the pastry in place.

Line the inside of the pastry-lined tin with baking paper and fill with split peas, rice or other baking beans. Blind bake the pastry for about 20 minutes, or until the pastry is dry but not coloured. Remove the beans and paper and return the tin to the oven for about 5 minutes, until the pastry is a light golden blond colour. Remove from the oven and allow to cool.

Reduce oven to 160°C. Combine the spring onion filling with the tarragon and spread half the mixture on the bottom of the pastry case. Crumble over half the goat's cheese, add the remaining spring onion filling and top with the rest of the goat's cheese. Pour over the cream mixture.

Bake the quiche for around 1 hour, then cool completely. To serve, trim off the pastry edges and remove from the tin.

Pizza perfection

Try using the Italian 00 flour, also known as pasta flour, to make these pizzas. You could use plain flour but I reckon extra-fine and high-gluten 00 flour is best if you like a lovely crispy base.

I cook my pizzas on the barbecue using a pizza stone – just try using a good pizza stone on your barbecue, and you'll never dream of having a wood-fired oven again! You can also cook them on a pizza stone in a conventional oven – they'll take around 10 minutes in a very hot, preheated 250°C oven.

I find that rolling the bases on baking paper makes them easier to handle as you move them to and from the pizza stone. Makes 5 pizza bases; the recipes opposite make enough topping for 1 pizza

500 g Italian 00 flour, plus extra for dusting
7 g sachet dried yeast
1 teaspoon salt
1 tablespoon olive oil
350 ml tepid water

To make the dough, combine the flour, yeast and salt in a mixing machine with a dough hook. Add the olive oil and enough warm water to make a soft but not too sticky dough. Mix on medium speed for about 10 minutes, or until smooth and elastic. Cover with a damp tea towel and leave to prove until doubled in volume.

Preheat your barbecue to 250°C, with the cover down, and place the pizza stone directly over the heat source.

Knock back the dough by kneading it a few times. Divide the dough into five evenly sized balls.

Spread out some baking paper and dust with flour. Roll out the bases on the paper until they're about the thickness of a 20-cent coin. Don't worry about the overall shape – I like them to be irregular.

When you've added your topping (see opposite), transfer the pizza bases to the pizza stone, leaving them on the baking paper – don't worry about the paper burning. Close the lid of the barbecue, and cook for 5–8 minutes, until the pizza is crisp and the topping is cooked.

Seafood pizza

2 garlic cloves, finely chopped

100 ml olive oil

3 tablespoons tomato passata

1 tablespoon capers

6 raw prawns, peeled and deveined

6 scallops, cleaned

1 squid tube, cut into thin rings

1 tablespoon chopped dill

1 tablespoon chopped flat-leaf parsley leaves

1 tablespoon chopped basil

¼ cup pitted black olives

1 teaspoon dried Italian mixed herbs

1 tablespoon grated parmesan

salt

freshly ground black pepper

Combine the garlic and olive oil. Brush the pizza base with the garlic oil, and spread the tomato passata evenly over the top. Scatter with capers.

Combine the seafood with the chopped fresh herbs and arrange on the pizza base. Sprinkle with the olives, dried herbs and parmesan. Season with salt and pepper.

Chorizo and smoked mozzarella pizza

2 garlic cloves, finely chopped

100 ml olive oil

3 tablespoons tomato passata

½ red onion, finely sliced

100 g dry-cured spicy chorizo, thinly sliced

100 g salted or fresh ricotta

100 g smoked mozzarella, roughly torn

small handful of wild rocket

sherry vinegar, to taste

Combine the garlic and olive oil. Brush the pizza base with the garlic oil, and spread the tomato passata evenly over the top. Scatter with onion and chorizo, and dot with ricotta and mozzarella.

While the pizza is cooking, combine the rocket and sherry vinegar to taste. When the pizza is ready, scatter with the dressed rocket.

Spinach and avocado salad with sesame dressing

This simple, Japanese-inspired salad goes really well with Caramelised Miso Beef (page 56).

Serves 4 as a side dish

200 g baby spinach

1 ripe avocado, sliced

2 French shallots, finely sliced

1 teaspoon sesame seeds, toasted

Dressing

⅓ cup rice wine vinegar

⅓ cup mirin

2 tablespoons lime juice

1 teaspoon wasabi paste

1 tablespoon sesame seeds, toasted and ground

1 tablespoon tamari

½ teaspoon sesame oil

⅔ cup sunflower oil

To make the dressing, place all the ingredients in a blender and mix until combined.

Wash and drain the baby spinach well. Toss the spinach with half of the dressing and arrange on a platter. Scatter the slices of avocado and French shallots over the top.

Pour over the remaining dressing and garnish with the sesame seeds.

Chowder

I generally see pipis in fishermen's bait boxes for catching whiting. They are easily found on most beaches and when purged of sand they are delicious. You can wash them in repeated changes of seawater.

Remember, it's best to cook these molluscs quickly to avoid making them chewy. If you don't fancy the hunt and labour of collecting your own pipis, buy some clams or mussels. For the white fish, look for fish that's soft and flakes – snapper or ling would be good. Serves 4

1 kg pipis, purged

750 ml dry white wine

80 g butter

1 leek, white part only, diced

2 sticks celery, diced

250 g sweet-cured streaky bacon, diced

2 potatoes, diced

2 tablespoons plain flour

½ bunch of thyme

600 ml cream

1 lemon

salt

freshly ground black pepper

100 ml clarified butter (see page 67)

2 handfuls of cubed stale bread

1 garlic clove

500 g diced white fish

2 tablespoons chopped flat-leaf parsley leaves, to serve

Cook the pipis in batches by warming the white wine and steaming them for about 2 minutes, until they're just open. Discard any pipis that haven't opened. Remove the meat from the shells, keeping the liquid and meat separate.

Melt the butter in a non-stick saucepan over medium heat. Add the leek and celery and gently cook for 10 minutes, without colouring, until soft and sweet. Reduce the heat to low–medium, add the bacon and potatoes and cook for 10 minutes, until translucent.

Sprinkle the bacon and vegetables with the flour and cook for 2 minutes. Add the thyme and gradually pour in the pipi liquid, stirring continuously, until you have a smooth, slightly thick soup.

Cook over low heat for 5–8 minutes, or until the potato is tender, then add the cream. Adjust the seasoning with a touch of lemon and salt and pepper.

To make the croutons, place the clarified butter in a small saucepan and heat over medium heat. When hot, add the clove of garlic. When the garlic starts to colour, fry the cubes of stale bread until just golden. Drain and season with salt and pepper.

When ready to serve the chowder, add the diced fish and simmer for 3–5 minutes, until the fish is cooked. Add the pipi meat just before serving – make sure you only just warm it through for 1–2 minutes.

To serve, garnish each bowl with the croutons and chopped parsley.

everyday

meals

beef

Pepper steak and stilton pie

Caramelised miso beef

Bender's beef burger

Ma po tofu

Calf's liver with silverbeet and
    blue cheese sauce

Kangaroo carpaccio

Herb crusted roast beef

Veal cotoletta

Mexican braised beef short ribs

Spag bolo sauce

Pepper steak and stilton pie

I've always had a love affair with the humble pie, so much so that in 2006 I started a pie business called the Great Australian Pie Company with a couple of guys in the UK.

This pie is not your classic Aussie pie but it's a wonderful combination to warm the cockles on a winter's day or night. The right kind of meat is essential, so use diced chuck, flank or brisket for the fullest flavour. Serves 4

1 kg braising beef, trimmed of excess fat and cut into large chunks
2 garlic cloves, chopped
small bunch of thyme
1 tablespoon black peppercorns
440 ml can Guinness
90 g plain flour, plus extra for dusting
salt
freshly ground black pepper
¼ cup sunflower oil
8 French shallots, halved
500 g puff pastry, defrosted if frozen
100 g stilton, crumbled
1 egg, beaten, to glaze

Place the beef, garlic, thyme, peppercorns and Guinness in a bowl. Cover and place in the refrigerator for 2–3 hours (or preferably overnight) to marinate.

Season the flour with salt and pepper. Remove the beef from the marinade, pat dry and toss in the seasoned flour. Strain the marinade and reserve the liquid.

Heat the sunflower oil in a large casserole. Add the beef in batches and brown all over – you want it to colour, not stew.

Remove the meat from the casserole and put aside. Brown the shallots in the casserole, then add the beef and reserved marinade liquid. Cover and simmer for about 1½ hours, or until the beef is tender. Alternatively, you could cook the beef in a 160°C oven for about the same length of time. When cooked, allow to cool slightly.

Preheat the oven to 200°C.

Place the puff pastry on a lightly floured sheet of baking paper and roll out to the thickness of a two-dollar coin. Sprinkle the stilton over one half of the pastry, fold the other half on top and roll out once again to the thickness of a two-dollar coin.

Make four lids for your pies by placing 4 individual pie dishes upside down on the pastry and cutting out circles. You could also use one big pie dish for this recipe. Spoon the filling into the pie dishes, brush a little beaten egg around the rims and top with the pastry. Trim the edges then brush more beaten egg over the top to glaze. Bake for 20–25 minutes until the pastry is crisp and golden.

Caramelised miso beef

I love this dish! The sweet saltiness of the marinade combines perfectly with the buttery texture of the Wagyu beef, which just melts in the mouth.

I have served this dish on its own as a canapé, and as a starter, accompanied by Spinach and Avocado Salad with Sesame Dressing (page 50). The inclusion of Wagyu beef makes this recipe a little out of reach for everyday occasions, but sometimes you can find it at a good price. If not, just look for some good grain-fed fillet. Note that if you're using the Wagyu, go for the middle cut so it has an even thickness. You'll find crispy shallots at Asian food stores and shizu cress at good greengrocers.

You probably won't use all of the marinade, but it will keep for up to 1 month in the refrigerator if stored in an airtight container, and it also freezes really well. Serves 10

1 × 1.5 kg fillet Wagyu beef
2 tablespoons crispy fried shallots, to garnish
shizu cress (optional), to garnish

Marinade
250 g red miso paste
175 ml mirin
75 g caster sugar

To make the marinade, combine the ingredients and place them in a glass bowl suspended over a simmering saucepan of water. Leave to simmer for 1 hour, or until the caster sugar has completely dissolved.

To cure the beef, firstly trim the fillet of all silver skin and external fat. Smear the meat well with the marinade. Cover and refrigerate for at least 2 hours, and up to 4 hours.

Line the grill tray with foil and preheat the grill to high. Spoon on any marinade that's drizzled from the beef, returning as much as possible onto the meat. Grill the beef for 2–3 minutes on each side until the marinade starts to caramelise.

Remove the beef from the grill and leave to cool to room temperature. Keep covered with foil until required.

To serve, thinly slice the beef and arrange on a platter. Garnish with crispy shallots and shizu cress (if using).

Bender's beef burger

I love a burger! When I'm asked what my greatest weakness is when it comes to food, I have to admit I'm a sucker for a certain well-known brand of burgers, though mainly when I'm feeling lazy or hung over!

This recipe was inspired by a little treat we used to make for ourselves when I was sous chef under Stuart Kennedy at Goodfella's in Newtown, Sydney. The little burgers would be made with dinner rolls and offcuts of beef from the menu. The benefits of being a chef ...

I think the cut of beef is really what defines this burger. Hanger steak is very flavoursome, and when you make your own burgers you have control over what goes into your mince. Makes 6

750 g hanger or skirt steak, minced
1 cup chopped flat-leaf parsley leaves
2 tablespoons finely chopped capers
salt
freshly ground black pepper
brioche buns (see page 24), or other
    soft buns
Dijon mustard, to serve
½ cup tomato relish (see recipe opposite
    or use your favourite relish), to serve

Onion confit
40 g butter
1 garlic clove, crushed
sprig of thyme
3 large onions, sliced
salt

Béarnaise sauce
3 egg yolks
2 tablespoons tarragon vinegar
250 ml warm clarified butter (see page 67)
1 tablespoon chopped tarragon
salt
freshly ground black pepper

To make the burger patties, place the steak, parsley, capers, salt and pepper in a bowl and mix until well combined. Divide the meat into evenly sized balls and slap them into the palm of your hand until you have equally sized tight balls of mince. Pat them into round patties to fit the size of your burger buns. If you're making the patties in advance, refrigerate them until required, but make sure you take them out of the fridge 30 minutes before cooking.

To make the confit, melt the butter in a saucepan. Add the garlic and thyme and sweat for 2 minutes. Add the sliced onions and cook slowly for about 30 minutes, or until golden, soft and sweet. Season with salt and keep warm until required.

To make the béarnaise sauce, whisk the egg yolks and vinegar over a double boiler until thick and fluffy. Slowly add the warm clarified butter while whisking continuously. Add the tarragon, and season with salt and pepper. Keep at room temperature until required.

Cook the beef patties on your barbecue or under a grill to your liking. When cooked, season to taste.

To serve, toast the brioche buns on both sides. Spread the lids with Dijon mustard and the bottoms with tomato relish. Place a beef patty on each bun and top with the onion confit and béarnaise sauce.

Tomato relish

1 tablespoon sunflower oil

1 teaspoon yellow mustard seeds

12 fresh curry leaves

1 onion, sliced

1 garlic clove, chopped

1 teaspoon ground turmeric

1 teaspoon ground coriander

1 teaspoon black peppercorns

½ teaspoon ground cumin

2 whole cloves

½ cinnamon stick

1 fresh or dried bay leaf

1 cup brown sugar

1 cup cider vinegar

2 x 400 g cans whole tomatoes, drained

salt

Heat the oil in a saucepan over medium heat. Add the mustard seeds and curry leaves, and heat until the mustard seeds pop. Add the onion and garlic and quickly fry. Toss through the remaining spices and bay leaf, and cook for 2 minutes. Stir in the brown sugar, cider vinegar and tomatoes and reduce. Cook out until thick, jammy and sweet and sour. Season to taste.

'The cut of beef is really what defines this burger.'

Hanger steak is a very flavoursome piece of meat, and when you make your own burgers you have control over what goes into your mince.

Ma po tofu

I grew up on minced beef, cottage pie, bolognese, savoury mince served with mash and peas and, of course, meatballs and rissoles! If my mum had made us this dish for dinner, our consumption of beef would have been that much more interesting. Served with steamed rice, it's mmm yum! Serves 4–6

2 tablespoons sunflower oil
250 g beef mince
1 tablespoon finely chopped ginger
2 garlic cloves, chopped
2 spring onions, chopped
1 tablespoon chilli bean paste (toban jiang)
2 tablespoons dark soy
1½ tablespoons shaoxing rice wine
2 tablespoons cornflour
250 ml chicken stock (see page 190)
250 g silken tofu, diced
1 spring onion, sliced on an angle,
   to garnish
1–2 teaspoons dark sesame oil, to taste

Heat 1 tablespoon of sunflower oil in a wok and stir-fry the beef mince, stirring with a spatula until the meat is separated and cooked. Remove from the wok and drain in a colander.

Reheat the wok and add the remaining sunflower oil. Add the ginger, garlic and chopped spring onions and fry for 2–3 minutes.

Return the mince to the wok and combine. Add the chilli bean paste and combine. Pour in the soy sauce and rice wine and cook for 2–3 minutes.

Combine the cornflour and stock. Add to the mince mixture to thicken and cook for 2–3 minutes. If the mixture is too thick, thin with a little water. Add the tofu and gently stir. Take care, as the tofu is delicate.

To serve, place the ma po tofu in a serving bowl, garnish with the spring onion and add sesame oil to taste.

Calf's liver with silverbeet and blue cheese sauce

I think calf's liver has suffered an injustice at the hands of mums, grandmothers and school dinner ladies for far too long! It's a shame that we have steered away from using offal – it's cost effective and good for you, and when done right, bloody tasty.

I cooked up this recipe on *The Best in Australia* for the 'best bang for your buck' challenge. It was beaten by 4 kilos of chicken wings cooked by Anna. The judges obviously made their choice based on volume! You could serve this dish with Balsamic Shallots (page 144). **Serves 4**

bunch of silverbeet
salt
2 tablespoons olive oil
1 garlic clove, crushed
freshly ground black pepper
100 g gorgonzola dolce
50 g mascarpone
2 tablespoons marjoram
100 g butter
½ cup plain flour
500 g calf's liver, cut into 1 cm slices

Separate the silverbeet leaves and thick white stems. Cook the stems in boiling salted water for 10 minutes, or until soft. Remove from the pan and chop. Cook the leaves separately for about 5 minutes, or until tender, then drain.

Heat the olive oil in a saucepan over medium heat and sauté the garlic until lightly golden. Add the silverbeet leaves and stems and gently sauté for about 5 minutes. Season, and keep warm until ready to serve.

Melt the gorgonzola and mascarpone in a small saucepan or over a double boiler. When melted, stir in 1 tablespoon of chopped marjoram, then keep warm.

Season the flour with salt and pepper and dredge the liver slices in the seasoned flour.

Melt the butter in a large frying pan until foaming, then add the liver slices. Cook until browned on one side, then turn. Cook for a further 4–5 minutes, or until medium cooked. Remove from the pan and rest.

To serve, divide the silverbeet between four plates and dress with a drizzle of the cheese sauce. Top with the slices of liver, add the remaining cheese sauce and sprinkle with chopped marjoram.

Kangaroo carpaccio

Kangaroo has largely been overlooked as a real alternative to beef. Though I doubt it will ever threaten to overtake the consumption of beef or lamb at the Australian family table, I think it deserves to be eaten for at least one meal every other week.

The only real problem with kangaroo is the irregularity of the size and shape of the cuts. I think it suits being served raw or rare, as it has a very low fat ratio, which can lead to it being dry and tough when overcooked. The creaminess of the goat's cheese really lifts this dish, and it's lovely served with crusty bread. Serves 4–6

250 g kangaroo loin
1 tablespoon chopped thyme
salt
freshly ground black pepper
2 tablespoons olive oil
watercress, to garnish

Confit
½ punnet red and ½ punnet yellow
    cherry tomatoes, halved
1 garlic clove, chopped
small bunch of thyme, chopped
pinch of dried chilli flakes
salt
freshly ground black pepper
70 ml extra-virgin olive oil
red wine vinegar

Dressing
80 g soft goat's cheese
juice of 1 lemon
100 ml extra-virgin olive oil
salt
freshly ground black pepper

Preheat the oven to 120°C.

To make a confit, line a baking tray with baking paper. Arrange the halved tomatoes in a single layer and sprinkle evenly with the chopped garlic, thyme and chilli flakes. Season liberally with salt and pepper and add a drizzle of extra-virgin olive oil. Place the tray in the oven and bake for 30–40 minutes, or until the tomatoes are semi-dried. Remove from the oven and leave to cool. When cool, place the tomatoes in a bowl and dress with a dash of vinegar and 50 ml extra-virgin olive oil.

Roll the kangaroo loin in the chopped thyme, salt and pepper. Allow to rest at room temperature for 30 minutes.

Heat the olive oil in a hot frying pan and sear the meat on all sides for 2–3 minutes, without cooking through. Remove the meat from the pan, cover with foil and leave to rest.

To make the dressing, mash the goat's cheese with the lemon juice. Add the extra-virgin olive oil while mixing with a spoon to create a loose dressing, then season with salt and pepper.

To plate up, cut the loin across the grain into thin slices. Using the side of a large knife, flatten the slices and arrange them on a large serving platter. It's a nice touch to leave gaps between the pieces of meat for presentation. Scatter with the tomato confit, drizzle with the dressing and garnish with a little cress.

Herb-crusted roast beef

Roast beef is one of those dishes that can warm the soul at the mere mention of the words. Though it's much more of an English tradition, it's something I grew up on as a child. Every Sunday there'd be roast beef for dinner, *The Winners* on the ABC and Yorkshire puddings to accompany the beef.

I have left the Yorkies out of this recipe but included the best beef accompaniment in the world, and the first I learnt to master as a young chef – béarnaise sauce! This method is easy and reduces the labour of whisking, though it's a little more in-depth than the version that accompanies Bender's Beef Burger (page 58). It's exactly like making mayo, the proper way to make it, as I learnt when I was a kitchen hand on Rottnest Island 23 years ago! Serves 6–8

1 x 2.5 kg rib-eye beef (grass-fed if possible)
2 tablespoons sunflower oil
bunch of thyme
bunch of rosemary
bunch of sage
100 g soft butter
fine rock salt
freshly ground black pepper
1 large onion
1 head garlic

Béarnaise sauce
300 ml clarified butter (see recipe opposite)
3 French shallots, finely diced
1 cup dry white wine
½ cup white wine vinegar
1 tablespoon chopped tarragon leaves, plus stems
5 black peppercorns
3 egg yolks
salt
freshly ground black pepper

Take the beef out of the fridge about 1–1½ hours before cooking.

Preheat the oven to 180°C.

In a heavy-bottomed pan, heat the sunflower oil until hot. Pan sear the rib-eye well on all sides until evenly coloured. Remove from the pan and place on a plate or baking tray to rest.

Wash the herbs well and drain. Spread out a piece of butchers twine on your bench or board; it needs to be long enough to wrap and tie around the beef. Place the moist herbs along the length of twine.

Smear the beef with the butter and season well with rock salt and pepper. Place the beef on the herbs and tie the twine around it so the herbs encase the meat. Secure any remaining herbs to the beef with more pieces of twine.

Wash and slice the onion, skin and all, and place it in a roasting tin, along with the broken-up and lightly squashed head of garlic. Place the herb-wrapped beef on top and roast in the oven for 60 minutes.

While the beef is cooking, prepare the béarnaise sauce. First, make the clarified butter (see recipe opposite). Pour the clarified butter into a small saucepan and keep hot on a very low heat.

Place the shallots, wine, vinegar, tarragon stems and peppercorns in a saucepan and simmer until reduced by two-thirds. Strain, then keep the reduction hot.

Place the egg yolks in a jug. Using a hand-held blender, blend the eggs with the hot reduction until foaming and light in colour. Slowly pour in the hot clarified butter, until a thick, creamy sauce develops. Season with salt and pepper and add the chopped tarragon leaves. Reserve and keep warm to serve with the sliced roast beef.

After the beef has been cooking for 60 minutes, check the internal temperature; for medium–rare it should be about 50°C. If the temperature is below 50°C, check after 5 minutes until the desired temperature is reached.

Once cooked to your liking, remove the beef from the oven and leave to rest in a draught-free place for 20–30 minutes. Serve with the béarnaise sauce.

Clarified butter

500 g butter

Slowly melt the butter in a microwave or small saucepan until the milk and fat have formed two layers. Skim any foam from the surface, then pour off the clear fats – this is the clarified butter – and throw away the milk solids.

Veal cotoletta

This dish was so popular when I used to cook it at Monte's in London. I also cooked it on *The Best in Australia*, and it won! It might have something to do with the funky crumbing mix of cornflakes and parmesan. It's a simple combination of flavours but it works really well. Serves 4

4 × 180 g veal rib-eye steaks
4 cups cornflakes
100 g parmesan, finely grated
1 cup plain flour
1 egg
200 ml milk
100 g butter
2½ tablespoons sunflower oil
12 sage leaves
8 anchovy fillets
bunch of wild rocket, to garnish

Salsa
1 large red capsicum
2 ripe tomatoes
1 small garlic clove, chopped
1 tablespoon chopped basil
salt
freshly ground black pepper
2½ tablespoons red wine vinegar
100 ml extra-virgin olive oil

Place the veal steaks between sheets of baking paper and beat until they're each around 3 mm thick.

Crush the cornflakes into fine crumbs in a mortar with a pestle. Combine with the parmesan.

In a separate bowl, combine the flour, egg and milk and whisk to a smooth batter.

Dip the veal into the batter, allowing the excess batter to drip off. Dredge in the cornflake and parmesan crumbs. To ensure that the veal is well coated with crumbs, pat it between your hands. Place each crumbed steak on a tray while you crumb the remaining veal cotolettas.

To make the salsa, grill the capsicum until charred, then allow to cool. Remove the skin and seeds, then dice. Blanch, skin and deseed the tomatoes, then dice. Place in a bowl and combine with the diced capsicum. Add the garlic and basil. Season with salt and pepper, then add the red wine vinegar and olive oil.

Heat a frying pan large enough to fit two of the cotolettas. Add 50 g of butter and the sunflower oil. When the butter starts to foam, add the veal and cook until crisp and golden on both sides. Remove from the pan and cook the remaining cotolettas.

Clean the pan, then add the remaining butter and heat until it starts to foam. Add the sage leaves and anchovies, allowing the sage to become crisp and the anchovy to soften.

Place the cotolettas on plates and dress with the sage and anchovy butter. Scatter with the salsa, and garnish with a little wild rocket.

Mexican braised beef short ribs

I love the flavours of this Mexican-style dish. Chipotles, or smoked jalapeno chillies, give a wonderfully earthy, smoky quality to the meat. You can buy them at good European delis, either in a can or jar with tomato sauce, which I prefer for this recipe, or as dried loose chillies. Using beef ribs is really cost effective – you can shred the leftovers and freeze the meat with the extra sauce, then use it to put together a tasty nacho-style sauce. Serves 4–6

12 beef short ribs
flour tortillas
sour cream, to serve
2 limes, cut into wedges, to serve

Marinade
6 chipotle chillies in adobo sauce
1 garlic clove, chopped
1 cup orange juice
½ cup lime juice
400 g can diced tomatoes, drained
2 tablespoons dried wild oregano
½ teaspoon ground cumin
2 tablespoons white wine vinegar
2 teaspoons salt
½ teaspoon freshly ground black pepper

Hot chilli sauce
6 habanero chillies, or 8–10 very hot red
   chillies (remove the seeds if you prefer
   a milder flavour)
1 large onion, chopped
400 g can diced tomatoes
½ cup white wine vinegar
1 tablespoon salt

Coriander salsa
2 tablespoons chopped coriander leaves
10 spring onions, thinly sliced on an angle
1 green capsicum, finely chopped
juice of 1 lime
freshly ground black pepper

Purée the marinade ingredients in a food processor, then transfer to a large shallow roasting dish. Add the beef ribs to the marinade, turning to coat. Cover with foil and leave to marinate in the fridge for at least 4 hours.

Preheat the oven to 160°C.

To cook the ribs, place the covered roasting dish in the oven and leave to cook for 3 hours, until very tender. The sauce should be thick; skim off any fat. When cooked, keep the ribs warm.

To make the hot chilli sauce, combine the ingredients and bring to a boil over medium–high heat. Reduce the heat to medium–low and simmer for 30 minutes, stirring occasionally, until thick. Cool slightly, then purée using a hand-held blender.

To make the coriander salsa, combine the coriander, spring onions and capsicum in a bowl. Pour over the lime juice and season with pepper.

Warm the tortillas in a hot oven or grill them until soft, then wrap them in a tea towel to keep warm.

To serve, present the beef ribs on a large dish accompanied by the tortillas and bowls of hot chilli sauce, sour cream and coriander salsa, with lime wedges on the side. The idea is for everyone to pull the meat off the bones and combine it with pieces of tortilla, some salsa and chilli sauce to make delicious mouth-sized parcels.

spag bolo sauce

Bolognese is a recipe that you must have in your repertoire. It's a 'please all people' type of dish. Even Herb, my oldest boy and fussiest eater, loves it.

If you like, you can add extra grated vegetables to the mix so you know your family is eating healthy food. It's also awesome on top of a pizza! I like to make this sauce in big batches so I can freeze it and have emergency meals ready to go. Serves 4–6

1 kg beef mince
salt
freshly ground black pepper
2½ tablespoons olive oil
1 large carrot, finely diced
2 sticks celery, finely diced
1 large onion, finely diced
3 garlic cloves, finely diced
1 glass red wine
3 x 400 g cans diced tomatoes
sprig of rosemary

Take the mince out of the fridge an hour prior to cooking, to take the chill off it; this will help you sear it.

Break up the mince by hand and season with salt and pepper. Cover and put aside.

Heat the olive oil in a large heavy-bottomed saucepan over medium heat. Add the diced carrot, celery, onion and garlic and cook gently for about 10 minutes, or until soft and translucent. You will need to keep an eye on it and stir regularly as you don't want the vegetables to burn or colour too deeply.

Push the vegetables to one side of the pan and add the minced beef. Cook for 3–4 minutes, allowing the meat to seal, before combining with the vegetables. Sauté for another 3–4 minutes, then give the mix another stir. You want the meat to be thoroughly sealed and incorporated with the vegetables.

Add the wine and reduce until the liquid has almost evaporated. Add the tomatoes and rosemary. Bring to the boil, then turn down to a simmer. Cook for about 1½ hours, or until the sauce is thick and rich.

lamb

Vietnamese lamb chops London style

I first ate these lamb chops in London, at a Vietnamese restaurant on the Kingsland Road, just up from the intersection of Old Street, Hackney Road and Shoreditch High Street. There are some great Vietnamese restaurants around there. I asked the chef for the recipe but he said no way, so this is my 'improved' version. In case you want to track it down, the restaurant is called Song Que. Serves 4–6

1 tablespoon ginger paste (see page 78)
1 teaspoon garlic paste (see page 78)
1 teaspoon ground turmeric
1 tablespoon sugar
⅓ cup shaoxing rice wine
12 lamb shoulder or neck chops
50 g vermicelli rice noodles, to garnish
1 carrot, grated, to garnish
½ cucumber, sliced, to garnish
¼ iceberg lettuce, shredded, to garnish
1 large sprig of mint, to garnish
¼ cup sunflower oil
1 onion, sliced

Nuoc cham
2 tablespoons caster sugar
2 tablespoons water
2 tablespoons fish sauce
juice of 2 limes
1 garlic clove, minced
1 birdseye chilli

To make the nuoc cham, whisk the caster sugar with the water. Add the fish sauce and lime juice, and stir to dissolve the sugar completely. Add the garlic and chilli and combine. Allow the sauce to rest for 1 hour before serving.

Combine the ginger and garlic pastes, turmeric, sugar and rice wine to make a wet paste. Rub the lamb chops thoroughly with the marinade and set aside.

Prepare the noodles, following the packet instructions. Arrange the noodles, carrot, cucumber, lettuce and mint on four plates. Top with the nuoc cham dressing.

Using either a large frying pan or the griddle plate of a barbecue, fry the lamb chops in the sunflower oil to medium–well done. Just before you remove the lamb, quickly fry the onion with the chops so it softens and picks up the flavour of the marinade and meat.

To serve, place the chops and onions on each plate next to the salad garnish.

Tamarind lamb chops

I cooked this on *The Best in Australia*. I absolutely love the flavours of this dish, and I also find it satisfying to make. The slow method of cooking the onions and spices with the potatoes gives it such depth of flavour. Plus, the final addition of tamarind, chopped chilli and mint gives the lamb a traditional flavour profile, but with the twist of spices! Serves 4

2 tablespoons sunflower oil

3 onions, thinly sliced

salt

1 tablespoon ginger paste (see page 78)

1 tablespoon yellow mustard seeds

1 tablespoon black mustard seeds

1 tablespoon ground coriander

½ tablespoon cumin seeds

½ teaspoon chilli powder

3 potatoes, sliced 1 cm thick

12 thick lamb chops

100 g tamarind paste

200 ml warm water

1 tablespoon chopped mint, to serve

1 large green chilli, chopped, to serve

Heat the oil in a large frying pan over medium heat. Add the onion and a good pinch of salt and fry for about 15 minutes, or until golden and soft.

Add the ginger paste and spices and fry for 2 minutes. Add the sliced potatoes and combine well with the onion and spice mixture. Continue to cook the potato and onion over low heat for 5 minutes, turning frequently, until the onion is a deep golden brown and the potatoes are cooked.

Move the potato and onion to one side of the pan, or remove completely. Add the lamb chops and cook until they are coloured and cooked to your liking. Return the potato and onion mixture to the pan and combine.

Combine the tamarind paste and water, then squeeze until the paste has dissolved. Discard the seeds and pulp. Add the tamarind to the lamb and potato mixture and mix well to heat through.

To serve, transfer to a platter and sprinkle with the chopped mint and green chilli.

Rogan josh

My love of Indian food began when I moved to East London. I discovered this recipe in an old regional cookbook given to me by an Indian chef who did a stint with me at Monte's in London, where I was head chef. I've used cottage cheese in my recipe, rather than the more traditional curd, as it's easy to find. Rogan josh is best served with naan bread and something to cool your mouth down, like a good mango chutney. Serves 4

4 lamb shanks, French trimmed
2 teaspoons garlic paste (see recipe below)
2 teaspoons ginger paste (see recipe below)
2 teaspoons ground turmeric
3 fresh bay leaves
175 g French shallots or small onions, finely sliced
⅓ cup sunflower oil
6 green cardamom pods, crushed
1¼ tablespoons freshly ground fennel seeds
½ teaspoon ground ginger
4 red scotch bonnet or small red chillies
100 g cottage cheese
¼ cup canned diced tomatoes

Preheat the oven to 180°C.

Mix the lamb shanks thoroughly with the garlic and ginger pastes, turmeric and bay leaves. Leave to marinate while you prepare the other ingredients.

Gently fry the shallots in 2 tablespoons sunflower oil until soft and translucent. Add the cardamom pods, fennel seeds and ground ginger. Cook gently for 5 minutes until aromatic.

Purée the chillies with 2 tablespoons sunflower oil. Add the shallot mixture, cottage cheese and tomatoes, then purée until smooth. Add to the marinated meat with 300 ml water and combine.

Place all the ingredients in a large saucepan; it needs to be big enough to hold the lamb shanks, with the sauce covering the meat but not the bones. Cover with wet baking paper and foil.

Place in the oven and cook for 2 hours, or until very tender. Check the liquid from time to time and top up with a little water if necessary.

Garlic or ginger paste

You can buy ginger and garlic paste, but it's easy to make your own. Make the paste in batches and freeze it in ice-cube trays.

200 g garlic cloves or ginger, peeled
sunflower oil

Place the peeled garlic or ginger in a food processor and blend with enough sunflower oil to make a smooth, lump-free paste.

Classic roast leg of lamb

I think some of the best lamb I have ever experienced has been cooked by Greeks. So, in order to embrace their flavours and add a few of my own, I generally combine the saltiness of anchovies with the classic Greek combo of lemon, garlic and oregano, with just a touch of dried chilli thrown in for good measure.

Cooking lamb over coals is the best way to enjoy these delicious beasts. Coal fires start hotter and slow down as they cook, so that's why I start off with a high heat and then lower it during the cooking process. Serves 4

1 x 2 kg leg of lamb, hipbone removed
8 anchovy fillets, broken into thirds
8 large kipfler or linska potatoes, washed
    and thickly sliced
1 onion, thickly sliced
1 bulb garlic
1 tablespoon chopped rosemary

Lemon marinade
3 garlic cloves, peeled
1 tablespoon dried Greek oregano
1 dried chilli
juice of 1 lemon
1/3 cup olive oil

To make the lemon marinade, pound the garlic, oregano and chilli in a mortar with a pestle. Add the lemon juice and olive oil.

Make about 25 incisions 3 cm in length in the surface of the lamb leg with a small sharp knife. Do not remove any fat. Using your hands, rub the leg of lamb with the lemon marinade and push it into the cuts. Stuff the pieces of anchovy into the incisions. Leave to rest for 1 hour.

Preheat the oven to 200°C.

Arrange the slices of potato and onion in a roasting tin. Break up the garlic clove and remove excess skin. Toss with the rosemary and add to the roasting tin. Position the lamb on top of the vegetables and place the tin in the oven.

Roast the lamb for 15 minutes, then reduce the heat to 160°C. Roast for another 40 minutes, then reduce the heat to 120°C and roast for a further 20 minutes.

Once cooked, allow to rest for 20 minutes before carving.

Tandoori leg of lamb

I cook this leg of lamb on my Big Green Egg barbecue. A regular barbecue set up for indirect cooking would be perfect, and it will also work well in a regular oven. When barbecuing, the addition of woodchips adds a lovely smoky flavour to complement the spices. Serves 4

1 × 2 kg leg of lamb, hipbone removed
¼ cup harissa
¼ cup plain yoghurt
juice of 1 lemon
salt
2 tablespoons coriander seeds

Brinjal
1 litre sunflower oil
2 eggplants, cut into large cubes
3 onions, thinly sliced
salt
1½ tablespoons ground coriander
½ tablespoon ground cumin
½ tablespoon ground turmeric
1 tablespoon ginger paste (see page 78)
1 tablespoon garlic paste (see page 78)
⅓ cup canned diced tomatoes
2 tablespoons white wine vinegar
freshly ground black pepper
2 tablespoons chopped coriander leaves

Preheat the oven to 250°C.

Using a small sharp knife, make crisscross cuts about 1 cm deep in the surface of the lamb leg.

Combine the harissa, yoghurt and lemon juice in a small bowl. Season with salt if required. Smear the paste all over the leg of lamb, then sprinkle with the coriander seeds.

Position the lamb on a wire rack in a roasting tin and roast for 45 minutes. Reduce the oven to 120°C and roast for a further 15 minutes.

While the lamb is cooking, make the brinjal. Heat the oil in a wok and, in batches, deep-fry the eggplant until golden and soft. Remove and drain on paper towel.

Remove all but around 3 tablespoons of oil from the wok and reheat. Add the onion and season with a teaspoon of salt. Fry for 5 minutes, until soft and starting to brown. Add the spices and ginger and garlic pastes and fry for a further 2–3 minutes. Add the chopped tomatoes and combine. Add the drained eggplant and fold together. Turn off the heat and season with vinegar, salt and pepper. Sprinkle over the chopped coriander and leave to settle.

When the lamb is cooked, allow to rest for 20 minutes. Serve with the brinjal.

Slow-roasted vodka lamb shoulder

Served on toasted sourdough, this is the perfect dish for lunch. It's quite rich, so the addition of the gremolata is a great way to lighten it up. A simple wild rocket salad dressed with lemon juice and olive oil would be the ideal accompaniment. Serves 6

1 × 2 kg lamb shoulder, easy-carve or shoulder blade removed
12 prunes, pitted
2 large sprigs of rosemary, broken and leaves removed
2 tablespoons olive oil
100 g butter
1 onion, chopped
1 celery heart, chopped
2 garlic cloves, thinly sliced
2 fresh or dried bay leaves
2 × 400 g cans diced tomatoes
1 tablespoon sweet paprika
150 ml vodka
2 cups chicken stock (see page 190), or beef stock

To serve
1 loaf sourdough
2 garlic cloves, peeled
olive oil
2 tablespoons chopped flat-leaf parsley leaves
zest of 1 lemon
salt
freshly ground black pepper

Preheat the oven to 160°C.

Make incisions in the lamb shoulder with a small knife and stuff with the prunes and rosemary. Heat the olive oil in a large pan over medium heat, and sear the shoulder on all sides. Set aside to rest.

Clean the pan and melt the butter. Add the onion and celery and cook over medium heat to soften. Add the garlic and bay leaves, followed by the tomatoes, paprika and vodka. Allow to cook for about 5 minutes.

Place the seared leg of lamb in the pan so you have a snug fit, then add the stock. Cover with a loosely fitted piece of baking paper. Place in the oven and cook for 2½–3 hours, until the meat is well cooked and the sauce is thick.

Cut thick slices of sourdough and grill in a ridged pan on both sides. Rub with a clove of garlic and drizzle with good olive oil.

Allow the lamb to rest for at least 30 minutes, then break into chunks and arrange over the toast.

Chop the remaining clove of garlic, then dress the lamb with some sauce, parsley, lemon zest, chopped garlic, salt and pepper.

pork

Cold roast pork with tuna mayonnaise

The Italians are masters of simplicity. This recipe is a twist on the classic dish vitello tonnato. It could be called maiale tonnato, which roughly translates as tuna pork! It's absolutely perfect for lunch on a hot summer's day, accompanied by a chilled glass of chenin blanc or cold-climate chardonnay.

We used to make this dish at the River Café in summer, using leftover roast pork. It's the perfect way to use up any leftovers if you've cooked a Cracking Roast Pork Belly (page 86). Serves 4

200 g roast pork belly or loin, crackle
   removed and chopped
4 kipfler potatoes, boiled and peeled
200 g green beans, blanched until tender
   and refreshed
2 tablespoons extra-virgin olive oil
juice of 1 lemon
salt
freshly ground black pepper
185 g can tuna in spring water
⅓ cup Japanese mayonnaise
8 anchovy fillets
1 tablespoon baby capers
¼ cup roughly chopped flat-leaf parsley
   leaves

Carve the pork into thin slices about 5 mm thick. Slice the cold cooked potatoes in half lengthways and trim the beans of their tops and tails.

Carefully place the pork, potatoes and beans in a bowl. Season with olive oil, lemon juice, salt and pepper.

Drain the canned tuna and break it up into a bowl. Combine with the mayonnaise and set aside.

To serve, arrange the pork, potatoes and beans in alternating single layers on a large, long platter. Spoon over the tuna mayonnaise and top with the anchovy fillets, capers and parsley.

Cracking roast pork belly

The popularity of pork belly has almost outstripped supply. Once the domain of the cheap-cut brigade, it is now a highly prized piece of meat. And rightly so, as the wonderful richness of the pork, the meltingly seductive juiciness of the fat and the crunch of a well-cooked crackle leave most people in a state of engorgement!

When cooking pork belly, more is much better than less. The leftovers can be used in so many ways, including for Cold Roast Pork with Tuna Mayonnaise (page 85). If you can, pre-order the pork belly and ask for it to be cut from the rib end of the whole belly, rather than from the soft, boneless stomach end, as you can use the bones to make excellent stock. Also, ask the butcher to hang it for a day so the skin dries out a little – this will help make a great crackle. If this isn't possible, just leave the pork belly uncovered in the fridge overnight, making sure nothing comes into contact with it.

Serve the pork and veg with some salsa verde (see recipe opposite) and a simple green salad of wild rocket and lemon juice. Serves 4–6

1 x 3 kg pork belly
1 tablespoon fennel seeds
1 tablespoon salt
2 bulbs fennel, outer layer removed
4 waxy potatoes, peeled
2 green apples
3–4 tablespoons olive oil
bunch of thyme
6 garlic cloves
salt
freshly ground black pepper

Using a small sharp knife, make cuts about 2 cm deep through the skin and fat of the pork belly and into the meat, as close together as possible. Place the fennel seeds and salt in a mortar and pound with a pestle into a fine powder, then rub into the cuts and skin of the pork belly. Set aside.

Preheat the oven to 180°C.

Slice the fennel into wedges, the potatoes into thick slices and the apples into thirds, removing the core. You want the pieces to be around the same size. Toss with a little olive oil to coat, and add the thyme and garlic.

Line a roasting tin with baking paper. Arrange the fruit and vegetables in an even layer, and season with salt and pepper.

Position the pork belly on top, then place the tin in the oven. Roast for about 20 minutes, to set the crackle, then reduce the heat to 160°C and cook for about 1½ hours.

Check the fruit and vegetables during the cooking time and give the tin a little shake so they cook evenly. If they are cooked before the pork, remove them from the tin and keep them to one side, rewarming to serve.

Salsa verde

1 cup flat-leaf or curly parsley leaves
1 cup basil leaves
1 cup mint leaves
1 cup rocket
2 tablespoons capers
6 anchovy fillets
1 garlic clove, peeled
1½ tablespoons white wine vinegar
½ tablespoon Dijon mustard
¾ cup extra-virgin olive oil
salt
freshly ground black pepper

Place the herbs in a food processor along with the capers, anchovies and garlic, and process until finely chopped. If necessary, add some or all of the vinegar to loosen the mixture.

Spoon the mix into a bowl and stir in the mustard and olive oil. Combine, then season with salt and pepper.

Allow the salsa to stand for about 30 minutes before using, and serve at room temperature.

The sauce will keep for up to 1 week in the refrigerator if stored in an airtight container.

Crispy pork and squid salad

This is my take on a flavour combination you see in many restaurants in Australia. I love the crunchy crispness of the fried pork and squid, and the fresh contrast of the herbs, fennel and cucumber. Keep the leftover stock as a base for soup – store it in a plastic bottle and refrigerate or freeze. Serves 6

1 × 1 kg pork hock, boned
4 spring onions, roots and tops trimmed
2 star anise
1 slice ginger
1 cup sunflower oil
100 g palm sugar
1 tablespoon tamarind paste
fish sauce, to taste
3 squid tubes, cleaned and cut into rings

Salad
1 bulb fennel, finely sliced and placed in
    iced water
1 Lebanese cucumber, finely sliced and
    placed in iced water
½ cup mint leaves
½ cup coriander leaves
1 kaffir lime leaf, finely sliced
1 small red chilli, deseeded and finely
    sliced

Dressing
juice of 1 lime
½ garlic clove, chopped
caster sugar, to taste
fish sauce, to taste

Preheat the oven to 140°C.

Place the pork hock, spring onions, star anise and ginger in a large saucepan, and add enough cold water to cover the meat. Bring to the boil, then turn down the heat to a simmer and cover. Place in the oven to braise for 3 hours. Once cooked, remove the pork hock from the stock. Remove any fat from the stock and allow to cool. Refrigerate or freeze for later use. When the pork is cool enough to handle, cut it into 2.5 cm cubes and set aside.

Prepare the salad by draining the fennel and cucumber and combining them with the herbs and chilli.

Make the dressing by combining the lime juice and garlic. Stir in the caster sugar and fish sauce to taste, then set aside.

Heat the sunflower oil in a wok over medium–high heat. When hot enough to cook a piece of bread golden brown in around 5 seconds, cook the pork in batches; you may need to top up the oil. Place a few cubes of pork in at a time and cook until crisp, crunchy and a dark golden colour. Be careful as the oil can spit. Drain the cooked pork on kitchen paper.

Drain the oil and return the wok to the heat. Add the palm sugar and bring to the boil. Return the pork to the wok and combine thoroughly, then mix in the tamarind. Season with fish sauce to taste, and keep warm.

Heat a griddle pan and quickly grill the squid. Add to the pork, tossing to combine. To serve, place the pork and squid on a platter. Dress the salad, and arrange on top.

Toad in the hole

My grandma made the best Yorkshire puddings. They're the perfect winter warmer. The secret to good Yorkies is hot fat, so be careful. You need four small earthenware or cast-iron dishes (such as Le Creuset), at least 5 centimetres deep, or you could also make it in a single baking or roasting dish. Place the dishes on a tray, just in case there's any spillage of hot fat.

These Yorkies are also great with Herb-crusted Roast Beef (page 66). This recipe may make more batter than you need, but it's better to have too much than not enough! You can make the gravy with powder or liquid. It's nice to have a bit of spinach on the side, but it's not essential. Serves 4

8 thick pork sausages
8 rashers streaky bacon
8 sprigs of rosemary
1 cup vegetable oil
freshly ground black pepper
1 large onion, sliced lengthways
50 g butter
1 garlic clove, chopped
salt
400 ml thick gravy

Yorkshire pudding
225 g plain flour
pinch of salt
3 eggs
200 ml milk
200 ml water

To make the Yorkshire pudding batter, combine all the ingredients and whisk well so the batter is thin and lump free. Allow to rest for at least 1 hour, ideally overnight.

Preheat the oven to 180°C.

Wrap each sausage with a strip of bacon and fasten with a sprig of rosemary.

Divide the vegetable oil between four ovenproof dishes, place on a baking tray and heat in the oven until just smoking.

When very hot, remove the tray from the oven and carefully place 2 sausages in each dish. Try to stack the sausages against each other, to give the dish a little height – don't worry too much about it though, it's just for effect!

Sprinkle with pepper, then pour over enough batter to cover two-thirds the depth of the sausages; you don't have to use all the batter.

Return the tray to the oven and cook for about 20 minutes. The Yorkshire puddings should rise and be crispy and golden brown.

To make the gravy, gently cook the onion in the butter until very soft and slightly golden. Add the garlic, season with salt and pepper, then add to the prepared thick gravy. Serve hot with the toad in the hole.

Pork and scallop egg nets

Egg nets are easy to make and a fantastic way to present a salad. Typically, they are used in Thai cuisine, as in this case. This combination also works well with leftover roast pork belly or loin.

I find non-stick Teflon barbecue liners are handy when making these egg nets, as the egg just slips straight off. I cook them on the barbecue but you could easily use a frying pan or wok. However you cook them, I strongly recommend using a Teflon liner or some lightly oiled baking paper. Serves 4

3 eggs
1 teaspoon chopped ginger
½ teaspoon chopped garlic
1 tablespoon sugar
2 tablespoons shaoxing rice wine
100 g pork fillet, thinly sliced
10 scallops, white meat only
2 cups bean sprouts, trimmed
¼ cup oyster sauce
4 spring onions, thinly sliced
2 small red chillies, sliced
bunch of coriander, leaves picked
½ bunch of mint, leaves picked
juice of 1 lime

Whisk the eggs in a large bowl until just combined. Strain through a fine sieve to remove the membranes and break down the protein. Cover and refrigerate.

Make a marinade by combining the ginger, garlic, sugar and rice wine. Place the pork slices in the marinade and marinate for 1 hour.

To make the egg nets, heat a Teflon barbecue liner or baking paper on the flat plate of your barbecue or in a large frying pan over low heat. Dip the end of a whisk in the chilled egg mixture and drizzle over the liner to form a crosshatch pattern or spider web effect. Once the egg sets, turn it out onto a large plate and cover with a sheet of baking paper. Repeat the process with the remaining egg mixture to make four egg nets. Place the egg nets on four plates.

Wipe the barbecue liner clean and place over a medium–hot barbecue plate. Place the pork slices on the liner and cook for 1 minute on each side, until golden, then set aside.

Wipe the liner and cook the scallops for 3–4 minutes, until golden, then place them in the bowl with the pork. Quickly fry the bean sprouts on the barbecue liner, until hot but still crisp. Combine the bean sprouts, scallops and pork, then toss through 1½ tablespoons of oyster sauce.

Make a salad by combining the spring onion, chilli, coriander and mint leaves. Dress with lime juice.

To serve, spoon the scallop and pork mixture into the egg nets and top with the salad. Fold over the egg nets and drizzle with the remaining oyster sauce.

Baked pork chops

I love a good pork chop, and I think it's important to source the best pork you can. In Australia there is a growing trend towards rare-breed pigs like long blacks, saddlebacks, Tamworths and Berkshires. The meat from these free-range rare-breed pigs has a superior flavour and texture to intensively farmed, often imported pork. Serves 6

6 pork loin chops
salt
freshly ground black pepper
small bunch of marjoram or oregano,
    leaves picked
zest and juice of 1 lemon
⅓ cup extra-virgin olive oil
1 head garlic, broken into cloves
2 × 400 g cans diced tomatoes
750 g yellow wax beans or green beans,
    trimmed

Preheat the oven to 200°C.

Season the pork chops with salt and pepper. Use a sharp knife to make cuts into the rind of each chop.

Heat a non-stick frying pan to very hot then cook the chops for 2–3 minutes on each side, until golden brown.

Place half the marjoram leaves, the lemon juice, a pinch of salt and 2 tablespoons of olive oil in a mortar and crush with a pestle into a rough paste.

Place the pork chops on a roasting tray and pour over the herbed oil paste. Sprinkle with half the lemon zest and throw in all but 2 of the garlic cloves. Roast for 20–30 minutes until the chops are well cooked and the skin is crackling.

Slice the remaining 2 garlic cloves. Heat 2 tablespoons of olive oil in a large frying pan over medium heat, add the sliced garlic and cook for 2 minutes. Stir in the tomatoes and cook for a further 10 minutes.

Arrange the beans on top of the tomatoes, cover with a piece of damp baking paper and leave to bubble gently for about 15–20 minutes, or until the beans have softened.

Stir the remaining lemon zest and marjoram through the cooked beans and serve with the pork chops.

My Mexican-style hot dogs

These barbecued beauties will set your day on fire! Be careful of the chilli sauce though – it's hot as Hades and should be approached with caution. The sauce will keep for several months in the fridge, and even longer if frozen. Just pour any leftover sauce into sterilised jars, put them in a saucepan of water and bring to the boil. Allow them to boil for 5 minutes, then turn off the heat and leave the jars to cool in the water. If you're not up to making your own sauce you can buy one, just make sure it's made with habanero chillies as they have a fantastic fruity and fiery character. What you really need to do though is get your hands on a decent rough-textured sausage with loads of flavour. Feeds 12

12 thick, coarse-minced pork sausage
12 soft hot dog rolls
1 cup sour cream, to serve
2 cups grated cheddar, to serve

Hot chilli sauce
1 tablespoon vegetable oil
1 small onion, chopped
2 garlic cloves, chopped
1 cup chopped carrot
10 habanero chillies
¼ cup lime juice
¼ cup white vinegar
1 teaspoon English mustard
1 teaspoon salt

Guacamole
2 avocados, halved and stone removed
juice of 2 limes
2 spring onions, finely chopped
250 g cherry tomatoes, halved
1 tablespoon chopped coriander leaves
salt
freshly ground black pepper

Coriander salsa
2 tablespoons chopped coriander leaves
10 spring onions, thinly sliced on an angle
1 green capsicum, finely chopped
juice of 1 lime

To make the chilli sauce, heat the vegetable oil in a frying pan over low heat. Gently sauté the onion and garlic until soft but not coloured. Add the chopped carrot, chillies, lime juice, vinegar, mustard, salt and 1 cup of water. Simmer until the carrot is soft. Place the mixture in a blender. Don't worry if you think the mix is too watery – it needs to have a bit of liquid. Blend until smooth.

Make the guacamole by using a fork to roughly mash the avocados in a bowl. Add the lime juice, spring onion, tomatoes and coriander. Season to taste and stir to combine.

To make the salsa, combine all the ingredients just before you're ready to serve.

To make up the hot dogs, slowly chargrill or barbecue the thick pork sausages. Slice the hot dog rolls lengthways and fill each one with a sausage topped with guacamole, salsa and hot chilli sauce. Add a dollop of sour cream and top with grated cheddar.

poultry

Apricot chicken

....

Family chicken curry

....

Quail bisteeya

....

Vegemite roast chicken

....

Coq au vin

....

Slow-roasted duck with sage and ginger

....

Chinese beer-can chicken

....

Chicken biryani

....

Chicken and mushroom pie

....

Apricot chicken

Here's another retro-style dish that deserves a revisit. Most quick recipes for apricot chicken use French onion soup and apricot nectar as a base, but I reckon you might as well get some good flavour happening by making an onion confit. It's a simple cooking technique and it's tasty! You could serve the chicken with Wet Polenta (page 141), White Bean Purée (page 140) or some mashed potatoes. Serves 4

4 chicken marylands, skin on
1 cup plain flour
salt
freshly ground black pepper
100 g butter
100 ml sunflower oil
½ bunch of thyme
3 garlic cloves, sliced in half
1 large onion, sliced
1 teaspoon coriander seeds
½ teaspoon ground cumin
400 g can apricot halves
1 cup chicken stock (see page 190)
1 tablespoon chopped tarragon

Remove the knuckle from the chicken leg and cut the maryland into two pieces, the thigh and the drumstick. Season the flour with a good pinch of salt and pepper and toss with the chicken pieces. Set aside.

Heat 50 g of butter and 50 ml of oil in a large heavy-bottomed saucepan. In batches, fry the chicken pieces in a single layer for 5 minutes on medium–high heat, until golden brown.

Remove the butter and oil from the saucepan, then wipe clean with paper towel, leaving any bits of caramelised chicken in the pan to add flavour. Melt the remaining butter and oil over medium–low heat and add the thyme, garlic and onion. Cook gently for 10–15 minutes, or until soft and golden brown. Season with salt and pepper.

Add the chicken and spices to the pan and cook for 3 minutes over low heat until aromatic. Pour in the apricot juice and stock and cover. Simmer for 30 minutes. Add the apricot halves and cook for a further 10 minutes.

Before serving, check the seasoning and stir in the chopped tarragon.

Family chicken curry

I love discovering the food of new cultures — especially when it's cooked for you! When we moved to Brisbane, we were introduced to some friends of friends. Ivor is Sri Lankan and his wife, Leigh, has learnt to cook the most amazing Sri Lankan dishes. Thankfully, she has allowed me to share one of her simple yet delicious curries with you.

I think the key to cracking these recipes is sourcing the spices — look for a good Indian or Sri Lankan food store. You can buy the curry powder already roasted. The pandanus leaf is optional, but boy does it make a difference! Serves 4–6

1 × 1.8 kg chicken, cut into 14 pieces
4 fresh curry leaves
3 stems lemongrass, bruised
4 pieces pandanus leaf (optional)
2 level teaspoons roasted curry powder
1 level teaspoon paprika
3 green cardamom pods, crushed
3 garlic cloves, chopped
2 tablespoons chopped ginger
1 onion, finely diced
½ cinnamon stick
¼ teaspoon ground turmeric
1 level tablespoon table salt
¼ cup white vinegar
½ cup coconut milk

Place all the ingredients except the coconut milk in a cold heavy-bottomed saucepan. Give it a good stir so all the pieces of chicken are well coated. Set aside for a few hours or for best results leave it overnight in the fridge.

When ready to cook, stir in 1 cup of water. Cover the saucepan and cook the curry over low heat for up to 1½ hours, stirring occasionally, until the chicken is white and cooked through. When cooked, add the coconut milk. Stir gently while it heats to almost boiling.

Turn off the heat and allow to stand for 10 minutes, covered, until ready to serve.

Quail bisteeya

In 2001 I spent four weeks filming in Morocco. Moroccan history runs deep and the country's food has been influenced by many cultures over the centuries, from Spanish and French to Jewish and Persian. The use of spices in Moroccan cooking is almost unequalled, achieving great subtlety and depth of flavour. The combination of sweet and savoury is quite profound!

Bisteeya is one of Morocco's iconic dishes, making great use of the signature sweet and savoury combination. Traditionally it's made with warka pastry, which isn't too dissimilar to filo, only thinner. To make things easier, I use filo, as do most Moroccans these days! Serves 4

½ cup crushed toasted almonds

½ cup crushed toasted pine nuts

2 tablespoons ground cinnamon, plus extra to serve

2 tablespoons icing sugar, plus extra to serve

8 sheets filo pastry

250 ml clarified butter (see page 67)

Filling

bunch of coriander, roots and tops separated and washed

3 garlic cloves, thinly sliced

sea salt

½ teaspoon ground ginger

1 teaspoon ground cumin

½ teaspoon ground turmeric

10 French shallots, thinly sliced

8 large quails, boned and split in half

5 eggs, lightly beaten

freshly ground black pepper

1 cup chopped flat-leaf parsley leaves

zest of 1 lemon

Preheat the oven to 180°C.

To make the filling, roughly chop the coriander roots and place them in a mortar or food processor, along with the garlic and 1 teaspoon of salt. Pound with a pestle or process to a paste, then add the ginger, cumin and turmeric and combine. Add the shallots and combine.

Place the split quails in a roasting tin and combine with the shallot and spice mixture. Pour in enough water to half cover the quails. Allow to marinate for about 2 hours; this isn't essential so don't worry if you don't have enough time.

Cover the tin with foil or baking paper and cook in the oven for about 20 minutes, or until the quails are just cooked and still a little pink.

Allow to cool, then place the quails on a chopping board. Remove any bones, then roughly chop the meat. Place the roasting tin on the stovetop over medium heat and cook until the liquid is reduced by a quarter, then return the chopped meat to the tin. Stir in the lightly beaten eggs and slowly heat until the mixture has thickened. Remove from the heat and allow to cool. Season with salt and pepper, then add the coriander leaves, parsley and lemon zest. The mixture should resemble perfectly scrambled eggs, and be quite thick and not watery.

Blend the almonds and pine nuts in a food processor, then combine with the cinnamon and icing sugar. Set aside.

Bisteeya is one of Morocco's iconic dishes, making great use of the signature sweet and savoury combination.

Preheat the oven to 180°C.

Layer 4 sheets of filo pastry in a 25 cm frying pan or baking tin, buttering each sheet with clarified butter. Place the layers so they face in different directions to cover all sides of the pan or tin. Sprinkle the fourth layer with the nut mixture. Repeat with another 4 layers of filo, once again sprinkling the fourth layer with the nut mixture.

Spoon the quail filling on top of the pastry, then fold back the overhanging edges of filo to create a closed top. You may need to add a few extra sheets of filo to seal the top. Press down firmly and brush the top layer of pastry with clarified butter. Place in the oven and bake for 30 minutes, or until golden and crisp. Allow to rest, then turn out onto a large serving plate.

To serve, sprinkle with icing sugar and cinnamon.

Vegemite roast chicken

This recipe is an Aussie take on roast chicken, using one of the most iconic Aussie foods there is – Vegemite! I use Vegemite as a stock base for a lot of things. When I first started making pies in the UK, I used it as a flavour base and colouring agent. However, when you end up needing 20 kilos of the stuff a week, it can get a little tedious opening jar after jar! Thankfully, you don't need that much for this recipe. The chicken juices make awesome gravy – just mash in the onions from the bottom of the roasting tin. Serve this with Palestinian Potato Salad (page 148) and some green beans. Serves 4

1 x 1.6 kg chicken
freshly ground black pepper
½ bunch of thyme
3 garlic cloves, peeled
¼ lemon
2 tablespoons Vegemite
2 onions, halved

Preheat the oven to 180°C.

Trim the excess skin and fat from the cavity and neck of the chicken. Season the inside of the chicken with pepper, then stuff the thyme, garlic and lemon into the cavity. Smear the Vegemite evenly all over the chicken.

Place the onion cut-side down in a roasting tin. Pour in 1 cup of water and place the chicken over the onions, with the breast facing up.

Place the tin in the oven and roast for 30 minutes. Turn the chicken, add a little more water and roast for a further 20 minutes.

To check if the chicken is cooked, insert a long knife into the thigh of the chicken: if the juice runs clear, the chicken is ready. Allow to rest for 15 minutes before carving.

Coq au vin

The classic recipes of the 1970s are back in fashion, and one of my favourites is coq au vin. Basically, it's chicken cooked in red wine with bacon, shallots and mushrooms. It's perfect served with a nice creamy mash, green beans and spinach. Serves 4–6

1 × 1.8 kg chicken or 8 chicken thighs, skin removed

4 sprigs of thyme, plus 2 tablespoons thyme leaves

250 g streaky bacon, cut into large squares

1 bulb garlic, peeled

3 fresh or dried bay leaves

10 black peppercorns

salt

1 tablespoon vegetable oil

20 g butter

150 g field mushrooms, peeled and cut into quarters or eighths

300 g Thai pink shallots, peeled

1 level tablespoon plain flour

1 tablespoon dried porcini mushroom powder

400 ml gamay or pinot noir

freshly ground black pepper

1 tablespoon chopped flat-leaf parsley leaves, to serve

If you're using a whole chicken, you need to joint it for sautéing. First remove the legs, cutting down through the skin between the legs and the main body of the chicken. Pull the legs outwards to pop the hipbones, then use the knife to separate each leg completely. Chop off the top knuckle where the feet would have been – this is called French trimming – then cut the legs in half at the joint between the thigh and the drumstick.

Next, use a large chopping knife to cut the ribcage section of the chicken away from the breast, leaving you with the two breasts still on the bone. Remove the wings at the first joint from the breast. Turn the breast over so the bones are facing upwards, and cut it in half along the breastbones. Cut these two sections in half. Finally, remove the skin from the chicken joints.

Place the jointed chicken in a large dish and combine with the sprigs of thyme, bacon, garlic, bay leaves and peppercorns. Lightly season with salt and allow to stand for 10 minutes.

Heat the vegetable oil in a large heavy-bottomed saucepan over low–medium heat. Add the chicken mixture and brown. Don't allow the saucepan to get too hot; it's better to cook the ingredients slowly. When the chicken begin to colour and the bacon starts to crisp, remove all the ingredients and reserve.

Add the butter, mushrooms, shallots and 2 tablespoons of thyme leaves, slowly cooking until soft. Return the chicken mixture to the saucepan and stir. Add the flour and mushroom powder and cook for 2–3 minutes. Pour in the wine and bring to a very gentle simmer. Cover and leave to cook for 45 minutes. (If you prefer, cook the casserole in a preheated 170°C oven for 45 minutes.)

Once cooked, remove from the heat and allow to stand for about 10 minutes. When ready to serve, adjust the seasoning if necessary, then sprinkle with the chopped parsley.

at home with ben

Slow-roasted duck with sage and ginger

Duck is one of my favourite poultry, and slow roasting is a sure-fire way of getting the best out of your bird. Due to the fatty nature of its skin, the meat stays moist even when well cooked. Using a whole bird will give you bones for making duck stock (see page 191) and leftover meat for other meals, such as Duck and Nutmeg Ravioli (page 197), extending your family budget.

    If you don't have a roasting tray large enough to hold the two ducks, you could use a large bamboo steamer instead. This dish is lovely served with some steamed spinach and White Bean Purée (page 140). Serves 4–6

2 x 1.8 kg ducks, neck and giblets removed
100 ml brandy
5 cm knob of ginger
6 garlic cloves, smashed with skin on
bunch of sage, leaves picked and stems reserved
1 tablespoon salt
100 ml sunflower oil

Preheat the oven to 180°C.

Trim the excess fat from around the ducks' cavities, as well as from the neck areas. Rinse the cavities with the brandy.

Chop half the knob of ginger and place in the ducks' cavities, along with the garlic and reserved sage stems.

Place a wire rack on the bottom of a large roasting tin; it needs to be big enough to hold the two ducks. Fill the tin with boiling water so it comes to below the top of the rack. Place the birds on top of the rack, cover with foil and place in the oven to roast for 1 hour.

Remove the ducks from the oven. Pour off and reserve the meat juices that have collected in the roasting tin. Use a table knife to scrape away the fat cells that have formed on the skin, and soak up the excess fat with paper towels.

Place half the sage leaves and the salt in a mortar and pound with a pestle to a paste. Rub this all over the ducks.

Return the ducks to the roasting tin, breast-side down on the rack but without any water in the tin. Reduce the oven to 160°C and roast for a further hour.

When it comes to buying poultry, it's worth spending a little bit more, both for the flavour and out of respect for the way the birds live.

After an hour, turn the ducks over and roast for a further 30 minutes. By this stage the legs should be very tender and the breasts well done but still moist, as the fat will have rendered and basted the meat during the cooking process. Remove the ducks to a carving board to rest.

Make a gravy by slowly simmering the reserved meat juices in a pan on the stovetop until reduced by half or three-quarters, skimming off any excess fat from the surface.

Heat the oil in a small saucepan over medium heat. Finely slice the remaining ginger into very thin slices and fry until golden brown and crisp. Remove and drain on paper towel. Add the remaining sage leaves to the pan, and fry until crisp. Drain on paper towel.

Carve the duck breasts from the bone and separate the legs. Serve the duck with the gravy, garnished with the sage and ginger.

Chinese beer-can chicken

A version of this recipe appeared in my first book, *Outdoor*. I love to experiment, and I've been playing around with different ways of barbecuing, using my new barbecue, the Big Green Egg. It's a modern version of a Japanese kamado oven, a traditional wood- or charcoal-fuelled earthenware stove. It takes cooking a chook on a beer can to a whole new level of sophistication!

This recipe is great served with steamed rice, bok choy and oyster sauce. You can freeze any leftover glaze and use it next time you cook up this recipe. You will need to buy yourself a beer-can chicken stand from a barbecue store. Serves 4

1 x 1.8 kg chicken
1 spring onion, halved
1 garlic clove, halved
1 star anise
375 ml can beer (Chinese, if possible)
¼ teaspoon sesame oil

Glaze
¼ cup light soy sauce
2 tablespoons dark soy sauce
2 star anise
1 stick cassia or cinnamon
6 thin slices ginger
½ teaspoon Sichuan pepper
25 ml shaoxing rice wine
50 g maltose or glucose

To make the glaze, combine the ingredients in a saucepan with 1 cup of water and simmer for 10 minutes. Remove the spices and set aside.

Hold the chicken by the neck over a bowl and use a ladle to pour the hot glaze over it. Place the chicken on a wire rack and leave to dry for 15 minutes. Repeat this process three more times. Ensure the chicken skin is evenly coloured; it will tighten and take on a well-tanned appearance.

Place the chicken in the fridge for 3 hours before cooking, leaving it on the rack to dry out.

Heat your barbecue for indirect cooking or preheat the oven to 200°C.

Push the spring onion, garlic and star anise into the opened can of beer. Place the can of beer in your beer-can chicken stand, then push the chicken onto the can of beer. Place the chicken and can on a tray and cook in the barbecue or oven for about 30 minutes.

Allow the barbecue to cool to 180°C degrees. This can be achieved quickly by opening the lid and turning the gas down. The Big Green Egg allows you to close off the airflow to lower the temperature. If you're using a conventional oven, reduce the heat to 180°C. Cook the chicken for another hour. When cooked, cover with foil and leave to rest for 30 minutes before serving.

To make a gravy, combine the juices from the chicken with a little glaze mixture and sesame oil.

'I love roast chicken.'

It's one of my favourite things to cook at home, and doesn't have to be boring at all. Try an Aussie take on the classic roast chicken by using Vegemite or a can of beer!

Chicken biryani

I have made many biryanis over the years, and included a vegetarian version in my first book, *Outdoor*. I love the flavours and the anticipation of what will be revealed when you lift off the lid and turn over the rice to expose the aromatic luxury of the meat and sauce beneath.

One of the finest biryanis I've ever eaten was cooked for me by a lovely couple from the Barossa Valley. It was studded with dried fruit, and since then I have included dried apricots in my version.

A cast-iron Le Creuset pot would be ideal for cooking this biryani. Serves 4

6 chicken thighs, bone in, skinned, jointed
    and cut in half
100 ml sunflower oil
2 onions, sliced
pinch of saffron
2½ tablespoons milk
5 green cardamom pods, crushed
1 stick cinnamon
5 whole cloves
3 fresh or dried bay leaves
75 g tomato paste
500 g basmati rice, washed and drained
1 cup chopped mint leaves
1 cup chopped coriander leaves
½ cup toasted cashews
½ cup chopped dried apricots
1 tablespoon garam masala, to serve
2 green chillies, chopped, to serve

Marinade
50 g ginger paste (see page 78)
50 g garlic paste (see page 78)
4 red chillies, puréed
150 g plain yoghurt
1 tablespoon ground turmeric

Combine the marinade ingredients. Add the chicken and leave to marinate for 2 hours in the fridge, or preferably overnight.

Preheat the oven to 170°C.

Pour the sunflower oil into a large heavy-bottomed ovenproof saucepan or casserole dish and shallow fry half the onion over medium heat until golden and a little crisp. Drain and set aside.

Place the saffron in the milk and set aside to soak.

Reheat the oil and add the cardamom, cinnamon, cloves, bay leaves and remaining onion. Fry until slightly golden. Add the chicken, reserving the marinade, and stir for 10 minutes over medium–high heat. Mix in the tomato paste and reserved marinade and simmer over low heat for 5 minutes.

Boil the rice until two-thirds cooked. Drain and arrange on top of the chicken, alternating layers of rice with the reserved fried onion and the chopped mint, coriander, cashews and apricots. Finish with a layer of rice.

Pour the saffron milk over the top of the biryani and cover with a tight-fitting lid. Place in the oven and cook for 20 minutes. When cooked, remove from the oven and allow to stand for 10 minutes before serving.

To serve, turn over the layers of rice with a spoon and sprinkle with the garam masala and chopped green chillies.

Chicken and mushroom pie

This is a classic pot pie, as it doesn't have a pastry base. It's more for the table than for eating on the run like a good old Aussie meat pie! Serves 4

100 g butter

500 g chicken thigh fillets, cut into large dice

2 eggs, hardboiled and sliced

200 g streaky bacon, rind removed

freshly ground black pepper

1 onion, thinly sliced

1 tablespoon chopped tarragon

1 tablespoon chopped flat-leaf parsley leaves

200 g field mushrooms (around 4 large mushrooms)

200 g puff pastry, defrosted if frozen

1 egg, lightly beaten, to glaze

Preheat the oven to 180°C.

Rub the bottom of an ovenproof pie dish with butter. Layer the dish with the sliced chicken, egg and half the bacon. Lightly season with pepper. Add a second layer of sliced onion, herbs and mushrooms and cover with the remaining bacon.

Roll out the pastry on a lightly floured piece of baking paper to about 2–3 mm thick, a little larger than the pie dish. Place the pastry over the pie dish and trim the edges. Brush the top of the pie with egg wash, and prick the centre so steam can be released. Place in the oven and bake for about 1 hour.

Remove from the oven and allow to stand for 10 minutes before serving.

seafood

Malay-style prawn salad

Last year I cooked a fortieth-birthday barbecue for an Aussie guy living in Singapore. There were around sixty guests, and I loved it. I spent the day before the event shopping in the markets and taking inspiration from the food for sale in the hawker centres. This is just one of the results of that experience.

The highlight was the tiny dried anchovy-like fish that were fried and served as a topping on different dishes. I knew this salad needed some crunch and saltiness so I grabbed some. You can get them here in Australia at Asian food stores. Serves 4–6

1 cup sunflower oil

50 g dried anchovies

¼ cup shredded or sliced coconut

100 g green beans, blanched until tender and refreshed

250 g cooked king prawns, peeled and deveined

1 spring onion, thinly sliced

1 cup Thai basil leaves

½ cup mint leaves

1 cup small betel leaves or watercress

¼ cup coconut cream

salt

Dressing

1–2 small red chillies

juice of 3 limes

2 teaspoons caster sugar

2 tablespoons fish sauce

Heat the sunflower oil in a wok over medium–high heat. When hot enough to cook a piece of bread golden in around 5 seconds, add the anchovies and fry until golden brown. Drain and set aside on paper towel until required.

Place the coconut in a frying pan and toast over medium heat for about 5 minutes, tossing all the time, until golden. Set aside to cool.

Trim the beans of their tops and tails, then chop. Pound half the prawns in a mortar with a pestle until coarsely shredded. Slice the remainder in half.

Combine the dressing ingredients in a large bowl and mix until the caster sugar has dissolved. Add the shredded and sliced prawns, green beans, toasted coconut, spring onion, Thai basil, mint and betel leaves or watercress. Combine well.

Season the coconut cream with a little salt, pour over the salad and serve straight away.

My Kids' favourite fish cakes

My wife and I have been making these fish cakes for our kids since we were living in the UK. They love them, even our middle child, Herb, who is the fussiest eater. In the UK we'd use hot smoked mackerel, as it was cheap and plentiful in London. It's a little harder to find in Australia, but hot smoked salmon or trout works really well instead. You need to pick through the fish thoroughly, to make sure there are no bones.

The difference between hot smoked and sliced smoked salmon is the smoking temperature. Hot smoked salmon is cooked using hot smoke, whereas regular smoked salmon is cured using smoke that is cool. Using hot smoked fish means this dish is just a little easier and quicker to put together, because the fish flakes very easily and the flavour is slightly stronger.

These fish cakes can be eaten cold, so they're great for kiddies' lunch boxes. We send Ruby to school with them, along with some sweet chilli sauce to dip them in. They're also delicious served with a cucumber and yoghurt salad. *Makes 20 small fish cakes*

500 g potatoes, peeled

500 g hot smoked mackerel, salmon or trout, bones removed

1 cup plain flour

2 eggs

1 cup milk

2 cups crushed cornflakes

200 ml sunflower oil

50 g butter

Boil the potatoes in salted water until tender. When cooked, drain and allow to steam dry, then mash.

Flake the fish with a fork, making sure there are no bones left in the flesh. Combine with the dry mashed potato. Using your hands, form the mixture into bite-sized potato patties.

Combine the flour and eggs in a bowl, then whisk in the milk to make a batter. You want the batter to have the consistency of pouring cream.

Dredge the fish cakes in the batter. Allow them to drain for a couple of seconds, then roll them through the cornflakes. Pat the crumbed fish cakes into shape, then place them on a tray lined with baking paper.

Heat the sunflower oil in a large frying pan over medium heat. Add the butter and when gently foaming, fry the fish cakes in batches so they are crisp and golden on all sides.

When cooked, remove and drain on kitchen paper. Allow the potato cakes to cool a little before serving.

Crispy hot and sour salmon salad

I cooked this salad quite often when my wife and I were living in London. It's a great light dish that's packed with flavour. Rather than cooking the salmon medium–rare, you need to really overcook the fish and get it crispy and crunchy. This develops a deeper flavour. You could also use another oily fish like mackerel. This salad goes really well with steamed rice. **Serves 4**

100 g cucumber, thinly sliced

bunch of spring onions, thinly sliced on an angle

2 French shallots, thinly sliced

bunch of coriander, washed and leaves picked

bunch of flat-leaf parsley, washed and leaves picked

½ birdseye chilli, finely chopped

½ cup cashews

100 ml vegetable oil

400 g salmon fillets

2 tablespoons capers in brine, drained

juice of 2 limes

fish sauce, to taste

To make the salad, combine the cucumber, spring onions and shallots in a large salad bowl. Mix in the coriander, parsley and chilli. Toast the cashew nuts by gently heating them in a small frying pan until they start to release their toasty aroma. Set aside.

Heat the vegetable oil in a wok over medium heat. Add the salmon skin-side down and cook until very crispy. Turn the fish over and remove the skin.

Break up the salmon with a fork or pair of tongs, and continue to cook until the fish is flaked and starting to crisp. Add the capers and fry until crisp. Remove the fish and capers from the wok and drain on paper towel.

To serve, dress the salad with the lime juice and a good splash of fish sauce. Add the crispy salmon, capers and toasted cashews and give it a toss.

Chilli mussels

If I had a dollar for every mussel I have debearded to cook this recipe, I would be living on a luxury tropical island. As an apprentice, I would clean about 100 kilos of mussels a week – in fact, I'm surprised I even wanted to put this recipe in the book. But they taste so good, I had to!

Most people will tell you if a mussel doesn't open, you shouldn't eat it. From my twenty-three years' experience I've found that, firstly, if the mussel is open and it doesn't close when you tap it, don't eat it. It's dead! I find that the mussels that don't open when you're cooking them tend to have stronger muscles than the ones that open first. If you leave the unopened ones in just a little longer, you'll find that they will open eventually and you can eat them.

See if you can source Kinkawooka mussels from Port Lincoln in South Australia for this dish. I've found them to be consistently great. Serve them with plenty of crusty bread and butter. Serves 4

50 g butter
3 garlic cloves, chopped
bunch of spring onions, whites chopped, green tops thinly sliced to garnish
1 kg live pot-ready mussels
400 g can diced tomatoes
375 ml can beer
3 long red chillies, chopped
freshly ground black pepper
salt
1 tablespoon chopped coriander leaves, to garnish

Heat the butter in a large heavy-bottomed saucepan over medium–high heat. When it begins to foam, add the garlic and chopped spring onions and cook for about 2 minutes, stirring to prevent the mixture from burning.

Add the mussels and stir well. Pour in the tomatoes, a good slug of beer and the chillies. Stir, then cover, and keeping the heat medium–high give the saucepan a shake to move and open the mussels as they cook. When the majority of mussels have opened, spoon them out into a large bowl to serve.

Bring the sauce to the boil and season with pepper and perhaps a little salt.

To serve, pour the sauce over the mussels and garnish with the spring onion tops and coriander.

Wasabi prawns

Sometimes perfection can be understated. This dish is a good example. A friend of ours cooked it one night at a dinner party, and I just loved the flavours. The combo may be a little clichéd, but man it works! The wasabi brings everything together.

I've added my own little twist with the addition of the kadayif pastry (shredded Turkish filo). It's really worth the effort of tracking down this pastry, as regular filo just does not work – it gets too greasy. A good Greek or Turkish grocery store should stock it, and I've even found it at an everyday supermarket. If you lived in Hackney, I could tell you to go to the Turkish shop on Wells Street!

If you like, you can use skewers to prepare the prawns, as it's a little easier to cook them. Serves 4

2 ripe mangoes (Kingston pride or Bowen varieties are best), peeled, stoned and diced
2 thick wedges watermelon, diced into 1 cm cubes
⅓ cup Japanese mayonnaise
1 tablespoon wasabi paste, or to taste
12 large raw king prawns, peeled and deveined, tail left on
½ packet kadayif pastry
2 cups sunflower oil
salt
freshly ground black pepper
2 tablespoons coriander leaves (optional), to garnish
1 red chilli, julienned (optional), to garnish
2 limes, halved (optional), to serve

Arrange the mango and watermelon on a serving platter.

Combine the mayonnaise and wasabi to taste – I use around 2 teaspoons – and arrange next to the fruit.

Smear each prawn with the remaining wasabi, or to taste. Lay out lengths of the pastry and roll the prawns in the strands.

Heat the sunflower oil in a wok or saucepan over medium heat. Fry the prawns for 2 minutes, then drain and season with salt and pepper.

Serve the prawns with the fruit and wasabi mayonnaise, as well as the coriander leaves, chilli and lime halves, if desired.

Whiting sandwiches

At Christmas some friends of ours came to stay with us on the Gold Coast. To celebrate, I bought some fantastic whiting fillets and served them as a little snack with ice-cold beer. As these whiting sandwiches are really small, they are great as a funky nibble. Serves 4

12 × 80 g whiting fillets, butterflied
1 cup self-raising flour, plus extra for dusting
12 small sage leaves
6 anchovies, halved lengthways
1 lemon
1 tablespoon capers, chopped
1 French shallot, finely chopped
1 tablespoon chopped flat-leaf parsley leaves, plus extra to garnish
1 tablespoon extra-virgin olive oil
1 litre iced soda water
2 cups sunflower oil
lime wedges (optional), to serve

Place the butterflied whiting fillets skin-side down on a chopping board. Lightly dust the fish fillets with flour. Make the whiting sandwiches by placing a sage leaf on one fillet, topping with half an anchovy then folding the fillets together to form a sandwich. Dust lightly in the flour.

To make a dressing, use a paring knife to cut the skin and pith from the lemon, leaving just the flesh. Cut out the individual segments – do this over a bowl so you catch as much juice as possible – and roughly chop. Add the capers, shallot and parsley to the segments, followed by the olive oil.

Make a batter by whisking in enough ice-cold soda water to the the self-raising flour to reach a thin, pouring cream consistency. Set aside and keep very cold. For the best results, you could do this at the last minute.

Pour the sunflower oil into a wok or deep-fryer and heat to 180°C, or hot enough to cook a piece of bread golden brown in around 5 seconds.

Dredge the fish fillets in the ice-cold batter. Gently wipe against the side of the bowl to remove excess batter, then slowly lower into the hot oil. Cook for 3–4 minutes, turning the fillets evenly so all sides are cooked. Remove from the oil and drain on paper towel.

Serve the whiting with the dressing and lime wedges (if using), and garnish with chopped parsley, if desired.

Crab and rocket linguine

This is one of my favourite pasta dishes. I first came across it in Cape Town, when it was cooked for me by an Italian surfer (yes, they do get waves in Italy!) in a funky share house overlooking Camps Bay. What caught my attention about his method was the frozen branches of basil he used to infuse flavour into the oil. It's a great way to preserve herbs when you have an abundance of them, and used like this their flavour is maximised.

You can buy the crabmeat already picked – check to make sure none of the shell has been left in the meat. You could also use chopped prawns or shrimps for an equally tasty result. I prefer linguine for this dish, but the type of pasta you use is really up to you. Serves 4

400 g dried pasta
100 ml extra-virgin olive oil
2 garlic cloves, chopped
½ teaspoon dried chilli flakes
1 branch of basil
4 large ripe Roma tomatoes, blanched, peeled, deseeded and roughly chopped
salt
freshly ground black pepper
250 g blue swimmer crabmeat
1 cup chopped wild rocket, plus extra to garnish

Bring a large saucepan of salted water to a fast boil and cook the pasta, following the packet instructions.

Heat the olive oil in a large saucepan over medium–low heat. Add the garlic and chilli and gently fry, stirring, until the garlic starts to stick to the spoon. Add the basil branch and fry for 1–2 minutes. Add the chopped tomatoes and gently simmer for 2–3 minutes. Season with salt and pepper.

About 2 minutes before the pasta is ready, add the crabmeat to the sauce and gently simmer. Sprinkle in the chopped rocket, allowing it to wilt into the crab sauce.

Drain the pasta, reserving a little cooking water. Remove the basil branch from the crab sauce, then toss the cooked pasta through the sauce.

Check the seasoning and serve garnished with rocket.

Prawn and zucchini spaghetti

This is one of my favourite pasta sauces. I cooked it on *The Best in Australia,* and although it didn't win I still think it's the best prawn pasta sauce around. When I was living in the UK I'd use cooked shrimps. You can't get them in Australia so I use the tail meat from tiger prawns instead.

When cooking pasta, it's important to note that you shouldn't drain the cooked pasta completely, as a little pasta water will help loosen the sauce and help it to coat the pasta. It also helps stop the pasta from clumping together before it goes into the sauce. Just make sure it's not too wet or you'll end up with noodle soup! Serves 4–6

3 zucchini, yellow or green or a mix of both
100 ml fruity extra-virgin olive oil
salt
freshly ground black pepper
2 garlic cloves, chopped
1 dried birdseye chilli, chopped
500 g prawn meat, chopped
200 g canned diced tomatoes
1 teaspoon finely chopped rosemary leaves
500 g spaghetti

Wash, halve and roughly slice the zucchini. Heat 2 tablespoons of olive oil in a saucepan over medium heat. Add the zucchini and gently fry until the edges just start to turn golden, but without colouring completely. Season with salt and pepper and add ¼ cup of water. Allow the liquid to evaporate while stirring and mashing the zucchini. When the liquid has evaporated, fry for about 1 minute. Repeat with another ¼ cup of water, stirring and mashing while the liquid evaporates then frying for a further minute or two. Repeat another three times. The idea is to slowly fry, steam and mash the zucchini five times all up, in order to enrich the flavour and break down the vegetables.

Add the garlic and chilli to the pan and cook for 1–2 minutes. Add the prawn meat and cook for about 5 minutes, stirring from time to time so the bottom doesn't catch. Make sure you control the heat – if the mixture starts to colour, turn the heat down. Add the tomatoes and rosemary, season with salt and pepper, then repeat the slow-frying process for a further 5 minutes.

Bring a large saucepan of salted water to a fast boil and cook the pasta, following the packet instructions. Spaghetti should take about 10 minutes to cook.

Just before the pasta is cooked and ready to drain, add the remaining olive oil to the sauce. Drain the pasta, reserving a little cooking water, combine thoroughly with the sauce and serve.

  at home with ben

Cajun fish in beer sauce

This recipe works really well with flaky fish. When I was an apprentice we used to cook it with cobbler, which is like catfish but better. It's getting harder and harder to find cobbler these days, and you don't see it on the east coast of Australia at all, so try using some nice big flathead fillets instead. Crispy fried onions and garlic can be bought from Asian food stores, but it's a good idea to dry your own thyme. Simply tie a bunch of thyme with string and hang it up until it's dry and crisp. The spice mix can be stored in an airtight container. I like to serve this with Lemon Rice (page 161). Serves 4

70 g butter
1 tablespoon sunflower oil
4 × 180 g flathead fillets
1 green chilli, chopped
100 ml beer
salt
freshly ground black pepper
200 g canned diced tomatoes
½ cup chopped coriander leaves,
    to garnish

Spice mix
1 teaspoon cayenne pepper
1 teaspoon smoked paprika
1 teaspoon crispy fried onions
1 teaspoon crispy fried garlic
1 teaspoon celery salt (see page 14)
1 teaspoon dried thyme

To make the spice mix, combine all the ingredients in a food processor and pulse. Place in a large bowl.

Place 20 g of butter and the sunflower oil in a non-stick frying pan, and heat over medium heat until the butter starts to foam.

Dredge the fish fillets in the spice mix, then carefully place them in the foaming butter. Cook for 2 minutes on each side. Before the fillets are cooked, remove them to a plate.

Add the chopped chilli and 1 teaspoon of spice mix to the pan, and fry for 1 minute. Deglaze with the beer, then cook until the liquid has almost completely reduced. Season with salt and pepper, then add the tomatoes and the remaining butter. Continue cooking until it is reduced by half, then add the fish to finish cooking.

Garnish the fish with chopped coriander and spoon on some sauce.

Kerala fish curry

Darren Simpson cooked this dish on *The Best in Australia*. Darren's a chef who cooks mainly Italian and French food, and he blew me away with his discovery of this dish. Thanks for the inspiration, Daz!

I have changed it a little, but the nuts and bolts remain. Darren mixed the tempering with the sauce, but I like to keep mine separate, and I think steaming the fish keeps it cleaner. You can use bought crispy fried shallots and garlic for this recipe. Serve the curry with rice. Serves 4

1 tablespoon sunflower oil
2 large onions, thinly sliced
1 teaspoon thinly sliced ginger
2 garlic cloves, thinly sliced
2½ tablespoons red chilli powder
¼ teaspoon ground turmeric
salt
freshly ground black pepper
2 tablespoons tamarind paste
2 cups chicken stock (see page 190)
4 x 200 g thick portions red emperor or
    other reef fish
1 tablespoon crispy fried shallots, to serve
1 tablespoon crispy fried garlic, to serve
sprigs of coriander, to garnish

Tempering
1 tablespoon sunflower oil
¼ teaspoon fenugreek seeds
½ teaspoon mustard seeds
handful of fresh curry leaves

Heat the sunflower oil in a saucepan over medium heat. Fry the onion until translucent, then add the ginger and garlic and sauté until soft.

Combine the chilli powder and turmeric with a few drops of water to make a paste. Add to the pan and fry over low heat until the oil separates. Season with salt and pepper, then add the tamarind paste and stock. Bring the sauce to a boil, then simmer to reduce by a quarter. Keep warm.

Steam the fish fillets in a steamer over medium–high heat until the flesh just starts to give and flake under the pressure of your finger. At this point it will be just cooked. Turn off the steamer and allow the fish to rest while you prepare the tempering.

To make the tempering, heat the sunflower oil in a small frying pan over medium heat. Add the fenugreek seeds and fry until fragrant. Add the mustard seeds, and when they start to splutter, add the curry leaves and fry until crisp.

To serve, pour the sauce over the fish, followed by the tempering mixture. Sprinkle with the crispy fried shallots and garlic, and garnish with coriander sprigs.

Barbecued fish Vietnamese style

Traditionally, this recipe would have been cooked over a charcoal fire, a split piece of bamboo acting as a clamp to hold the fish over the coals. As most of us cook on a gas barbecue these days, it's best to use a fisharoo to prevent the fish sticking to the grill, and to help lift it up so it cooks via radiant heat. A fisharoo is a fish-shaped wire cage, which you can find at good barbecue supply shops.

This recipe works best with an oily type of fish. Ask your fishmonger to scale and gut it for you. Serve it with the nuoc cham sauce, some steamed rice and a salad. Any leftover sauce will keep for up to two weeks in the fridge if stored in an airtight container. Serves 4–6

1 × 1.2 kg oily fish, such as kingfish, queenfish or small Spanish mackerel, scaled and gutted

Spice paste
3 cm piece ginger
3 garlic cloves
3 French shallots
½ teaspoon ground turmeric
1 tablespoon fish sauce
juice of 1 lime
100 ml sunflower oil
½ cup fresh curry leaves

Nuoc cham
5 tablespoons caster sugar
¼ cup water
⅓ cup fish sauce
juice of 3 limes
1 large or 2 small garlic cloves, finely minced
1 long red chilli

To make the nuoc cham, whisk the caster sugar and water together. Add the fish sauce and lime juice, and stir to dissolve the sugar completely. Add the garlic and chilli and combine. Allow the sauce to rest for 1 hour before serving.

Make deep cuts across the skin on both sides of the fish, about 1 cm apart.

Place all the spice paste ingredients except the curry leaves in a food processor and purée until smooth. Finely shred the curry leaves and combine with the spice paste. Massage the paste into the cuts on both sides of the fish. Place the fish in the fridge and leave to marinate for 30 minutes.

Preheat your barbecue for direct grilling on a high heat.

Place the fish in the fisharoo; you might need to trim the tail fins so it fits into the cage nicely. Place the fisharoo directly over the heat and cook evenly on both sides for about 10 minutes per side.

Serve with the nuoc cham sauce.

Olive and rosemary salt-crusted ocean trout

The trick to this recipe is the temperature of the fish when you take it out of the oven. It's an impressive dish to cook. The lemon, rosemary, parsley and fennel add flavour to the trout, while also preventing the salt from getting inside the fish and making it overly salty. If your oven is a standard domestic one, try cooking this dish on your barbecue using the indirect cooking method.

You could serve the trout with a simple green salad, steamed cold potatoes and mayonnaise flavoured with finely chopped basil. Serves 10

2 cups black olives

5 kg rock salt

2 egg whites, lightly whisked

1 cup chopped rosemary leaves

1 × 2.5 kg ocean trout, freshly gutted, gills removed

2 lemons, sliced

bunch of flat-leaf parsley

1 small bulb fennel, sliced

Preheat the oven to 180°C.

To prepare the salt crust, place the olives in a food processor, stones and all, and pulse to chop them. Transfer to a large bowl, then add the salt, egg whites and half the rosemary. Combine well.

On a baking tray large enough to hold the trout, use half the salt crust mixture to make a bed 2–3 cm thick in the shape of the fish. Place the trout on top. Stuff the remaining rosemary, the lemon slices, parsley and fennel into the cavity of the fish.

Cover the fish with a 2–3 cm layer of the remaining salt mixture. If need be, use scrunched-up foil to hold the salt in place. Place in the oven and bake for 30 minutes.

To check that the trout is cooked, place a small knife or roasting fork into the thickest part of the fish. Touch it to your lips and if it's very warm (45°C), the fish is done. Before removing the salt crust, allow the fish to rest until it is cool enough to handle.

Carefully remove the salt crust by sawing around the base of the fish with a serrated knife, being careful not to cut into the flesh. Lift off the top layer of salt crust; it may come away in one section or break into several pieces. Brush any excess salt off the fish with a wet pastry brush, and remove any excess from the cavity.

To serve, gently peel back the skin to reveal the flesh. Cut down the centre of the fish and remove the flesh in portions. It should be wonderfully moist and pink.

vegies

Gem squash curry

White bean purée

Wet polenta

Singapore eggplant

Sri Lankan chickpeas

Balsamic shallots

Palestinian potato salad

Salt-baked onions with truffled egg

Eggplant al forno

Avocado tempura agedashi

Farinata

Artichoke and potato cannelloni

Risotto bianco with mushroom

Lemon rice

My famous falafel

Gem squash curry

This recipe was inspired by a dish my wife and I used to order at one of our favourite restaurants in Whitechapel, London. It's really simple to put together and the flavours are just fantastic. The key is to use gem squash, also known as cricket ball squash.

Serve it as a side dish with roast or barbecued lamb. Serves 4

3 gem squash
salt
2 tablespoons vegetable oil
1 onion, sliced
3 garlic cloves, puréed
2 cm piece ginger, puréed
2 teaspoons ground coriander
1 teaspoon ground turmeric
3 ripe tomatoes, diced
freshly ground black pepper
2 tablespoons chopped coriander leaves,
   to garnish

Boil the whole squash in salted water until tender. Remove from the saucepan and leave to cool. When cool, cut in half and discard the seeds. Scoop out the yellow flesh and set aside.

Gently heat the oil in a heavy-bottomed pan. Add the onion and a pinch of salt and sauté until the onion is golden brown and soft. Add the garlic and ginger and gently fry for 1–2 minutes. Add the ground coriander and turmeric and fry until aromatic.

Stir in the diced tomatoes and cook until soft. Add the reserved gem squash and combine so the tomato and spice mixture evenly coats the vegetable's yellow flesh. Warm through.

Serve the gem squash curry warm with a grinding of black pepper and chopped coriander.

White bean purée

Dried beans are something that should always be in your cupboard. They are the best substitute for rice and potatoes, and they go well with meat, fish and poultry or as part of an antipasto or dip plate.

If you don't want to go to the trouble of cooking your own beans you could use canned ones. Just drain off the liquid and heat them prior to pulsing. You could also try borlotti beans for a variation to this recipe.

Chopped spinach or rocket can be added to the warm bean purée, and it's perfect served with grilled or roast lamb or beef. Serves 4

200 g dried cannellini beans, soaked
    overnight in plenty of cold water
2 sticks celery
1 tomato
3 garlic cloves
sprig of sage
1 tablespoon red wine vinegar
¼ cup extra-virgin olive oil
salt
freshly ground black pepper

Drain the beans and place them in a large saucepan. Fill the pan with cold water, covering the beans with at least 5 cm of water. Add the celery, tomato, garlic and sage. Bring to the boil, then turn down to a simmer. Cook the beans until their skins and texture are soft and creamy.

When cooked, remove the celery and sage and drain off most of the liquid. Pulse the bean mixture in a food processor or blend with a hand-held blender. You want a rough but creamy consistency.

Season with vinegar and olive oil, salt and pepper before serving.

Wet polenta

I find that polenta works as a fantastic substitute for mashed potatoes or pasta if you're serving a stew or a pasta sauce like bolognese. When I worked at the River Café in London, polenta was a regular feature on the menu in November, when the new crop of polenta would arrive.

There are a few different types of polenta, depending on the corn used and the coarseness of the grain, and some take longer to cook than others. The best results always come from the polenta that requires the most effort and time to cook! Serves 4–6

1 litre water
salt
100 g polenta
100 g unsalted butter
100 g parmesan, finely grated
freshly ground black pepper

Pour the water into a heavy-bottomed saucepan, season with salt and bring to the boil.

When the water is boiling, pour the polenta into the water in a fine stream and whisk in. Leave to cook at a low simmer for about 20 minutes, then whisk in the butter and cheese. Season with salt and pepper.

The polenta can then be kept warm in a bowl over simmering water until required. To prevent a skin forming, dot the top of the polenta with butter and cover with baking paper.

Singapore eggplant

I experienced this dish while feasting in a hawker centre in Singapore. I was so taken by the flavours that I recreated it as best I could! In Singapore, they make it with long, light purple eggplants, which are so creamy, but these can be hard to find in Australia, so just use the best quality eggplant you can get your hands on. Serves 4–6

2 cups vegetable oil
1 large purple or black eggplant, sliced into 3 cm cubes
4 garlic cloves
3 red chillies
1 large stem lemongrass
5 coriander roots, plus leaves to garnish
100 g sugar
100 ml rice wine vinegar
fish sauce

Heat the vegetable oil in a wok and fry the eggplant in batches until golden and soft. Remove and drain on paper towel.

Place the garlic, chillies, lemongrass and coriander roots in a food processor and purée.

Pour off the vegetable oil from the wok, leaving 2 tablespoons. Add the puréed mixture to the oil and fry for 2–3 minutes, until aromatic.

Add the sugar, allow it to melt and then add the vinegar. You want a well-balanced sweet and sour flavour. Add the drained eggplant and season with fish sauce.

To serve, garnish with coriander leaves.

Sri Lankan chickpeas

Our friends Leigh and Ivor serve this dish as a snack. In Sri Lanka it's known as cuddler. It's great as a side dish for a barbecue, and I've also served it with grilled squid or cuttlefish. Serves 4–6

1 tablespoon sunflower oil
1 teaspoon yellow mustard seeds
1 onion, finely chopped
10 fresh curry leaves
2 green chillies, chopped
small pinch of cumin
440 g can chickpeas, drained
handful of fresh mint leaves
handful of fresh coriander sprigs
1 lemon, cut into wedges, to serve

Heat the oil in a large frying pan over medium heat. Add the mustard seeds, cover with a lid and fry until they pop. Remove the lid and add the onion. Sauté until soft and translucent. Add the curry leaves, chilli and cumin, and sauté until the onion is golden brown.

Add the chickpeas to the pan and cook until any moisture has evaporated.

To serve, divide the warm chickpeas between plates and scatter with mint and coriander. Serve with wedges of lemon.

Balsamic shallots

These shallots are *agrodolce*, which means sweet and sour. Small, tender shallots work best. They go really well with Calf's Liver with Silverbeet and Blue Cheese Sauce (page 64), as well as most roast meats. Serves 4

200 g French shallots, peeled
100 g butter
100 ml water
3 long sprigs of thyme
100 ml balsamic vinegar
1 garlic clove, crushed

Place the ingredients in a saucepan. Cover and simmer for about 30 minutes, or until the shallots are soft and the balsamic, butter and water have reduced and become homogenous, but not separated.

'Eat
your
vegies.'

My wife and I happily eat vegetable-only meals. I just wish my kids would eat vegetables without screaming!

Palestinian potato salad

This salad is so simple and tastes great. I put chilli in it but it works just as well without it. Use a good boiling potato that will fluff a little, like a chat or desiree, and choose ones that are roughly the same size. Serves 4–5

600 g potatoes, peeled
salt
3 garlic cloves, chopped
1 birdseye chilli, chopped
150 ml extra-virgin olive oil
juice of 1 lemon
handful of chopped flat-leaf parsley
   leaves
freshly ground black pepper

Boil the potatoes in salted water until tender. Drain and allow to steam dry.

Add the garlic and chilli to the potatoes, then toss with the olive oil. Allow the potatoes to break up a little and roughen up.

Add the lemon juice and parsley, then season with salt and pepper and serve.

Salt-baked onions with truffled egg

I love this recipe. It's a great way to make a silk purse out of a pig's ear. I first saw something like this in the Italian region of Piemonte, in the town of Alba. I used to cook it at Monte's during truffle season, with shavings of white truffle.

The cheeses really add depth of flavour. Comté is a great melting cheese from France made from cow's milk, with a wonderfully fruity quality. **Serves 4**

4 large onions
rock salt
50 g butter
1 garlic clove, sliced
4 sprigs of thyme
1 tablespoon plain flour
200 ml milk
100 g taleggio, sliced
100 g parmesan, grated
100 g comté, sliced
salt
freshly ground black pepper
4 egg yolks
20 g fresh black truffle or 1 teaspoon
    white truffle oil

Preheat the oven to 150°C.

Leaving the onions whole and unpeeled, prick the tops with a small knife and place them in a small pan or roasting tin. Half cover with rock salt and bake until soft.

Remove the onions from the salt and allow to cool. Cut off the tops, reserving them as lids. Scoop out the centre of the onion, leaving 1–2 layers of flesh on the inside. Roughly mince the scooped-out onion.

Heat 50 g butter in a saucepan and slowly cook the minced onion, garlic and thyme until sweet and soft. Add the flour and stir into the onion mix. Slowly stir in the milk, then bring the mixture to the boil and allow to thicken. Cook over low heat for 5 minutes, then remove from the heat and add half the cheese. Return the pan to the heat so the cheeses melt. Season with salt and pepper.

Return the onion skins to the layer of salt, positioning them in the holes formed when they were baked. Half fill each onion skin with the onion mix. Top with an egg yolk and some freshly shaved black truffle or a few drops of truffle oil, then add more onion mix. Sprinkle each onion with a little of each cheese and bake for about 10 minutes, or until golden.

Serve on a bed of salt, ideally with a little freshly shaved black truffle sprinkled on top.

Eggplant al forno

Eggplants are such a versatile vegetable. Just be sure to choose ones that aren't too heavy, as they can be full of seeds.

This is the basic recipe for baked eggplants that I cook at home. They can be served as a vegie main, or as a side dish to accompany roast lamb. You could also top them with seafood during the last few minutes of baking, or pour some Spag Bolo Sauce (page 73) over the top. Serves 4

4 dark eggplants
salt
freshly ground black pepper
⅓ cup extra-virgin olive oil, plus extra to drizzle
2 garlic cloves, finely sliced
1 long red chilli
sprig of basil
2 × 440 g cans diced tomatoes
1 cup grated mozzarella
½ cup grated parmesan
⅓ cup capers
8 anchovy fillets
1 cup coarsely chopped fresh breadcrumbs
½ cup finely chopped fresh herbs (basil, tarragon and flat-leaf parsley are good)

Place the eggplants under a hot grill and cook until the skin is blistered and the flesh is very soft, turning them at least once to cook on both sides. Remove the eggplants from the grill and leave to cool. When cool enough to handle, remove the skin, keeping the flesh intact. Place the peeled eggplants on a wire rack to drain excess juice. Season with salt and pepper and a drizzle of olive oil.

Preheat the oven to 180°C.

Heat 2 tablespoons of olive oil in a saucepan over moderate heat. Add the garlic and chilli and gently fry until the garlic is sticky and golden. Add the basil and fry quickly for a minute. Add the tomatoes and season to taste with salt and pepper. Cook until reduced by half.

Place the eggplants in a baking dish. Cover generously with the tomato sauce, then top each eggplant with mozzarella, parmesan, capers and anchovy fillets. Place in the oven and bake for about 15 minutes, or until the cheese is golden and bubbling.

While the eggplants are baking, heat the remaining oil in a frying pan. Add the breadcrumbs and fry until crisp and golden. Drain while hot, toss with the chopped fresh herbs and season with salt and pepper.

Sprinkle the breadcrumbs over the eggplant and serve.

Avocado tempura agedashi

Like most Japanese food, this dish has a simple and harmonious combination of textures and flavours. Most commonly you would serve tofu with the dashi stock, but I think the addition of avocado works really well! Serves 4

4 avocados
2 cups iced water
1 egg
1 cup plain flour, plus extra for dusting
pinch of baking powder
2 cups sunflower oil
salt
freshly ground black pepper
⅓ cup finely grated daikon, to serve
4 sprigs of shizu cress, to garnish

Agedashi stock
2 sheets kombu
5 g bonito flakes
2½ tablespoons mirin
2½ tablespoons light soy sauce

Make the agedashi stock by placing the kombu and 350 ml of cold water in a saucepan. Bring to a simmer, then turn off the heat and leave to stand for 5 minutes. Remove the kombu, then bring the water to the boil. Add the bonito flakes, then turn off the heat once again. Leave for 10 minutes, allowing the bonito flakes to settle to the bottom of the pan. Pass the liquid through a fine strainer, add the mirin and light soy sauce and heat the stock gently.

Halve, peel and quarter the avocados and set them aside.

Combine the iced water and egg and mix well. Combine the flour and baking powder and add to the egg mixture, mixing in enough to just combine, leaving a few lumps in the batter.

Heat the oil in a wok. Dust the avocado quarters in a little flour, dredge in the ice-cold batter and place in the hot oil, two at a time. Fry for 2–3 minutes, until crisp but not too coloured. Drain on paper towel and season with salt and pepper.

To serve, place a tablespoon of daikon in four small Japanese bowls. Divide the agedashi stock between the bowls and top each with two pieces of tempura avocado. Garnish with shizu cress.

Farinata

For me, farinata is the ultimate nibbly bite. A cool drink and a plateful of these crispy chickpea crepes just can't be beaten. They also make a great addition to an antipasto platter.

If you're using a cast-iron pan, make sure it's well seasoned so it's as close to non-stick as possible. The success of this recipe depends on the temperature of your oven and the temperature of your pan – the hotter the better. Serves 4

150 g chickpea flour
salt
75 ml olive oil
100 ml light olive oil
200 g raw prawns, peeled, deveined and
   sliced in half
¼ cup rosemary leaves, tossed in olive oil
freshly ground black pepper

Sieve the flour and slowly mix in 2 cups of tepid water to form a thin batter, making sure it's completely free of lumps. Leave to rest for 1–1½ hours.

Preheat the oven to 250°C.

Just before you use the batter, add a good pinch of salt and the olive oil, making sure they're thoroughly mixed in.

Heat a large non-stick or cast-iron frying pan on the stovetop. When hot, carefully add enough light olive oil to cover the bottom of the pan. Pour in enough batter to form a thin layer. Sprinkle with the sliced prawns, rosemary leaves and a little pepper.

Transfer the pan to the oven and cook for 5–10 minutes, or until the edges are brown. The centre should be cooked and the bottom crisp. Use a spatula to remove the farinata from the pan.

To serve, cut the farinata into pieces, arrange on a large plate or board and sprinkle with salt.

Artichoke and potato cannelloni

I used to cook this cannelloni dish at Monte's in London, for the restaurant's vegetarian menu. Adding some freshly shaved truffle prior to baking is a nice touch, or you could drizzle on a little truffle oil instead. Serves 6

500 g Jerusalem artichokes, peeled or
   scrubbed
¼ cup olive oil
2 tablespoons chopped thyme
salt
freshly ground black pepper
2 x 400 g cans artichoke hearts
2 garlic cloves, peeled
2 cups cream
100 g English spinach, blanched, chopped
   and squeezed dry
100 g potatoes, boiled, peeled and diced
⅓ cup tomato passata

Pasta
500 g Italian 00 flour, plus extra for
   dusting
6 eggs
2 egg yolks
1 tablespoon olive oil

Topping
200 g crème fraîche
2 egg yolks
100 g parmesan, grated
100 g mozzarella, grated

Cut the Jerusalem artichokes into similar sized pieces. Pour 2 tablespoons of olive oil into a heavy-bottomed saucepan, add the Jerusalem artichokes and fry over medium heat for about 5 minutes, or until golden. Add the thyme and season with salt and pepper. Pour in 100 ml of water, cover the pan with a lid and braise the Jerusalem artichokes until they're soft but not completely broken down. The water should evaporate; if the Jerusalem artichokes are still hard, add a little more water and repeat the process.

Place half the artichoke hearts, the garlic cloves and cream in a small saucepan. Gently simmer until the liquid has reduced by half, then use a hand-held blender to purée the mixture to a smooth consistency.

Dice the remaining artichoke hearts and set aside.

Heat the remaining olive oil in a saucepan over medium heat and sauté the spinach for 2 minutes, or until wilted.

To make the filling, place the braised Jerusalem artichokes, sautéed spinach, boiled potatoes and diced artichoke hearts in a large bowl and combine. Add half the puréed artichoke hearts to the mixture and mix well.

Preheat the oven to 180°C.

Make the pasta dough by placing the ingredients in a blender and combining until the dough comes together. Turn the dough out onto a floured board and knead until smooth. Cover the dough in plastic wrap and allow to rest for 15 minutes.

I used to cook this cannelloni dish at Monte's in London . . .

Roll out the pasta dough into six 10 × 15 cm sheets. Place a line of filling along one end of each sheet, then roll up the pasta to make the cannelloni.

Grease a deep baking dish and line the base with the tomato passata. Place the cannelloni in the dish and cover with the remaining artichoke purée.

To make the topping, combine the crème fraîche, egg yolks and parmesan, then spread the mixture over the cannelloni. Sprinkle with the mozzarella and season with salt and pepper.

Place in the oven and bake for 20 minutes until bubbling and lightly golden.

Allow to rest for 10 minutes before serving.

Risotto bianco with mushrooms

The easiest way to cook a risotto is to first make a plain white risotto, or risotto bianco, and then wilt in the flavourings at the end. This allows you to judge the amount of other flavourings you need to add. A really simple combination would be to simply slice prosciutto over the top.

There are three types of risotto rice: vialone nano, carnaroli and arborio. The rice starts to sizzle when you cook it, a stage known as 'the rice is singing'.

Leftover mushroom mix can be frozen and used to make another risotto or a mushroom sauce. The leftover rice can be refrigerated and turned into Arancini (page 193). Serves 4–6

100 g butter
½ cup finely diced celery
½ cup finely diced onion
4 cups carnaroli rice
2 garlic cloves, sliced
1 cup dry white wine
3 litres chicken stock (see page 190), boiling
100 g parmesan, grated

Mushroom base
50 g dried porcini mushrooms
50 g butter
1 garlic clove, chopped
1 tablespoon chopped thyme
500 g field mushrooms, sliced
salt
freshly ground black pepper

To prepare the mushroom base, soak the porcini mushrooms in 2 cups of boiling water for 10 minutes. Drain, reserving 1 cup of the soaking liquid. Wash the porcini under cold water and squeeze dry.

Gently heat the butter in a saucepan until foaming. Add the garlic and thyme and sauté for 1 minute. Add the field mushrooms and sauté until soft and the excess moisture has cooked out. Add the porcini and ¼ cup of the mushroom soaking liquid. Simmer until the liquid has almost evaporated. Repeat until all the soaking liquid has been used. Season and set aside to cool.

To prepare the risotto, melt 50 g of butter in a large heavy-bottomed saucepan and add the celery and onion. Gently sauté for about 10 minutes without colouring. Add the rice and garlic and stir well to combine. Sauté for 3 minutes until the rice begins to sizzle. Add the white wine and cook until the liquid has evaporated. Add enough boiling stock to just cover the rice. Stir gently over medium heat until the stock has been absorbed. Repeat this process until you have used up all the stock; it will take 15–20 minutes. The rice should be just tender but retain some bite, and be creamy and silky.

Mix through enough mushroom mixture to flavour the risotto according to taste. The flavour of the rice should still be detectable. Remove from the heat and add half the parmesan and the remaining butter. Stir well, then cover and leave to rest for 5 minutes.

To serve, divide the risotto between six plates and top with parmesan.

Lemon rice

This simple Indian-inspired rice dish is fantastic served alongside a curry. Serves 4

¼ cup sunflower oil

1 teaspoon mustard seeds

2 teaspoons chana dal (also known as Bengal gram)

½ cup cashews

5 g fresh curry leaves

1 teaspoon ground turmeric

1 teaspoon asafoetida

1 teaspoon ground ginger

500 g pre-cooked rice

juice of 1 lemon

salt

freshly ground black pepper

½ cup coriander leaves, to garnish

Heat the sunflower oil in a saucepan over medium heat. Add the mustard seeds and chana dal and toast until they start to pop. Add the remaining ingredients, except the seasoning and coriander, and thoroughly combine.

To serve, season with salt and pepper and garnish with coriander.

My famous falafel

In London, all the local restaurants and kebab joints have signs out the front saying 'Time Out's best'! I love my falafel, so I am making my official 'unofficial' claim to fame for my recipe.

The secret to making falafel is to let the mixture ferment and develop flavour. I like to dip them in harissa or yoghurt as a snack, and I also put them in the kids' lunch boxes. Makes 20 falafel

2½ cups dried chickpeas, soaked for at least 24 hours in plenty of cold water

½ cup finely diced celery

½ cup chopped spring onion

1 tablespoon chopped flat-leaf parsley leaves

½ teaspoon ground turmeric

¼ teaspoon chopped chilli

1 teaspoon sesame seeds

½ teaspoon salt

freshly ground black pepper

1 egg

sunflower oil, for deep-frying

Drain the chickpeas. Combine all the ingredients except the egg and sunflower oil in a food processor and blitz until fine crumbs form. Add the egg and blitz for a further minute or two. Cover and refrigerate for at least 2 hours and preferably overnight.

Heat the sunflower oil in a saucepan or frying pan to around 170°C.

Mould the mixture into flat balls. You can use 2 soup spoons to do this, then use one of the spoons to scoop the balls into the hot sunflower oil.

Deep-fry until golden, then drain on paper towel.

dinner party show stoppers

Roasted rack of veal

Veal is neglected these days, but I think it's a great dish for special occasions. For many years it was deemed unethical, but it's much more ethically farmed these days – in particular, look for the excellent White Rocks brand. The meat's flavour is due to the fact that the calves are just weaned, and it is unbelievably tender.

This rack of veal would be great served with Balsamic Shallots (page 144) and White Bean Purée (page 140) to balance the richness of the meat. Serves 8

8-bone rack of veal
salt
freshly ground black pepper
¼ cup olive oil
2 garlic cloves, smashed
bunch of rosemary, leaves picked
bunch of sage, leaves picked
8 rashers short-cut streaky bacon, rind
    removed
2 large onions, cut into quarters
gravy granules (optional)

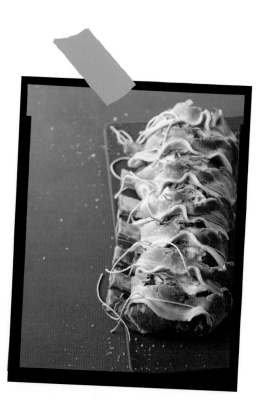

Rub the veal with salt and pepper, olive oil and garlic. Cover with the herbs, then wrap the rashers of streaky bacon around the veal to fill in the gaps between the bones. Tie with butchers twine to secure.

Preheat your barbecue for indirect cooking (outside burners on, the middle ones off) at about 250°C.

Line the bottom of a roasting tin with the onions, then pour over 1 cup water.

Place a wire rack over the onions, arrange the veal on top and transfer to the barbecue. Insert a barbecue thermometer and set for beef (medium–rare or however you prefer), pull the lid down and cook for 15 minutes.

Reduce the heat to 180°C and cook for a further 40–45 minutes. Keep the water level in the tin constant to stop the onions from burning; this liquid will become your gravy.

Remove the tin from the barbecue. Cover the meat with foil, and allow to rest for half the amount of cooking time.

While the meat is resting, place the roasting tin over medium heat on the stove top until the cooking juices are reduced by half. If you like, you can thicken the juices with gravy granules.

Carve each person a piece of veal with the bone attached and serve with the gravy and onions.

Vanilla and vodka cured trout

This is a delicious way to prepare ocean trout or salmon. Serve it with a simple rocket salad and some bread and butter. Serves 6

½ cup rock salt
½ cup brown sugar
1 vanilla pod
1 x 1 kg ocean trout fillet, cut from the thick part of the whole fillet, pin boned, skin on
¼ cup vodka
1 lemon
1 French shallot, finely chopped
1 tablespoon roughly chopped capers
1 tablespoon chopped dill
¼ cup olive oil
freshly ground black pepper

Place the salt and brown sugar in a food processor and pulse to combine well.

Split the vanilla pod lengthways. Reserve the split pod and smear the seeds over the flesh side of the trout.

Place the trout in a shallow dish, skin-side down. Sprinkle with the vodka and leave to cool in the fridge, covered, for 1 hour.

Combine the split vanilla pod with the salt and sugar mix and rub over the trout, pressing the vanilla pod into the skin. Cover the fish in plastic wrap and leave in the fridge overnight.

When ready to serve, remove the trout from the salt mixture – it will be quite wet by this stage. Wash off the remaining salt by running under cold water, then pat dry.

Using a sharp knife, carve thin slices of fish on an angle and arrange them on a serving platter.

Segment the lemon by using a small knife to remove the skin and pith. Cut out the segments, leaving the connecting membranes in place, then dice.

Scatter the shallot, capers, lemon segments and dill over the trout slices. Before serving, drizzle with the olive oil and add a grinding of black pepper.

Tagine of snapper

For me, this dish exemplifies Moroccan food: simple, flavoursome and spectacular!

Ask your fishmonger to gut, scale and fillet your fish, removing the spine and pin bones but leaving the head and tail attached. This will either challenge him and he will agree, or he'll say bugger off! You could cook it without doing the laborious deboning but it's worth the effort. Serves 4

2 x pink snapper or sea bream, filleted, head and tail attached
2 tablespoons olive oil
1 cup canned chickpeas
salt
freshly ground black pepper
½ cup crispy fried onions, to garnish

Marinade
2 garlic cloves
4–5 coriander stems, washed, roots and tops separated, tops chopped and reserved for garnish
1 teaspoon ground cumin
1 teaspoon chopped ginger
salt
400 g can diced tomatoes
juice of 1 lime
skin of 1 preserved lemon, finely diced
2 pinches of saffron
½ cup white wine

To make the marindade, pound the garlic, coriander roots, cumin, ginger and a little salt to a fine paste in a mortar with a pestle. Mix in the tomatoes, lime juice, preserved lemon, saffron and white wine.

Pour the mixture over the fish and marinate for 10 minutes.

Heat the olive oil in a tagine or heavy-bottomed saucepan over medium heat. Add the fish and marinade, along with the chickpeas. Bring to a simmer and cook for 10–15 minutes, continually spooning the sauce over the fish. You may need to turn the fish halfway through the cooking process.

Before serving, correct the seasoning and garnish with the crispy fried onions and reserved coriander tops.

Blue swimmer crabs with XO sauce

You can buy XO sauce, but it doesn't have enough dried scallops to make it true XO. Most of the ingredients for this recipe can be found at good Asian provedores. If you can't find Asian red shallots, just use normal French shallots. Serves 4

140 ml sunflower oil
250 g fresh egg or rice vermicelli noodles, cooked according to packet instructions
2 kg male blue swimmer crabs, cleaned
4 spring onions, whites and green tops separated and chopped
100 ml shaoxing rice wine
1 tablespoon cornflour

XO sauce
25 g dried salted fish, chopped (optional)
125 g dried scallops
75 g dried shrimp
50 g cured Chinese sausage
2 cups sunflower oil
75 g garlic, chopped
75 g red Asian shallots, peeled and finely chopped
50 g dried red chillies, broken up
1 tablespoon freshly ground black pepper

To make the XO sauce, soak the dried fish (if using) in several changes of water for 3 hours. Soak the dried scallops in water for 30 minutes, then simmer for 30 minutes, until soft. Drain, retaining the poaching water, and shred the scallops. Soak the dried shrimp in hot water for 30 minutes, then drain and mince. Dice the sausage and salted fish into 2 mm pieces.

When you're ready to make the sauce, heat the sunflower oil in a wok over high heat. Add the garlic, shallots and minced shrimp and cook until the moisture evaporates and the mixture begins to fry. Add the chillies, sausage and fish and cook until the chillies and sausage are translucent. Stir in the shredded scallops. Cook for 5 minutes, then add the pepper. Transfer to a food processor and pulse to roughly blend.

Clean the wok, then pour in 100 ml sunflower oil and heat over high heat. Add the pre-cooked noodles – leave them in the shape of a flat nest – and fry for 5 minutes, until crispy and golden, turning the nest to cook on both sides. Transfer to a serving dish and keep warm.

Heat the wok over high heat and add 2 tablespoons of sunflower oil. Add the crabs and stir-fry for 2 minutes. Add the whites of the spring onions, the rice wine and 100 ml of the scallop poaching water. Steam for 4 minutes. Add ¼ cup of XO sauce and steam for another 4 minutes until the crabs are cooked.

Combine the cornflour with ¼ cup of water to make a thin paste. Stir into the mixture to thicken the sauce.

To serve, pour the crab mixture and sauce over the noodles and garnish with the chopped green spring onion tops.

'I am obsessed with XO sauce.'

Whenever I go to Chinatown in Sydney, I have pipis in XO.

The history of XO sauce is relatively recent. It was first made in Hong Kong in the 1980s, and draws its name from the quality indicator of cognac. The high quality of this sauce is also indicated by the addition of dried scallops, which makes it expensive, but one batch will go a long way. Think of it as a labour of love!

Lobster thermidor

When I was an apprentice we used to sell lobster thermidor, Americana and mornay hand over fist! You don't see these dishes too often in restaurants these days but they still rock!

I cooked this dish on *Surfing the Menu* in Esperance, Western Australia, using a 3-kilo southern rock lobster. Very impressive but a little impractical – it's a little more manageable if you use four small live lobsters. Serves 4

4 x 600 g Western Australian rock lobsters
100 ml clarified butter (see page 67)
3 French shallots, finely chopped
100 ml cognac
600 ml thickened cream
2 tablespoons Dijon mustard
1 tablespoon English mustard
salt
freshly ground black pepper
4 egg yolks
2 lemons, cut into wedges, to serve

To kill the lobsters, place them in the freezer for about 10 minutes, until they're dead but not frozen. Plunge them into boiling water for 3 minutes – this will make the flesh pull away from the shell without cooking it. Pull the tail from the head of each lobster, then use a pair of kitchen scissors to cut the membrane from under the tail and remove the meat, twisting and pulling the final piece nearest the tail to remove the gravel sack.

Place the heads and tails in the boiling water to cook to a bright red colour – this will take around 5 minutes. When cooked, drain well. Use scissors to cut a section of shell from each lobster head, large enough for you to sit the tail in the hole securely. Arrange on a serving platter with the tails turned upwards.

Heat a non-stick frying pan over low heat and gently sauté the clarified butter. Dice the lobster meat, add it to the pan and very gently poach for about 3 minutes, until just starting to colour. Remove to a plate.

Preheat the oven to 200°C.

Discard most of the butter, then add the shallots and sauté over medium heat for about 5 minutes, until translucent. Turn up the heat and add the cognac. Flame and reduce by half.

Stir in 2 cups of the cream and reduce by half, then add the mustards and season with salt and pepper. Reduce the sauce until thick, then turn off the heat and add the lobster meat.

Combine the egg yolks and the remaining cream and season. Mix with the lobster meat and sauce and place over low heat until the sauce is thick enough to coat the back of a spoon. Check the seasoning again.

Spoon the lobster meat and sauce into the upturned lobster tails, then place in the oven to bake for 5 minutes, until bubbling and golden and dark in patches.

Serve with the lemon wedges.

Aromatic duck curry

I've cooked this recipe a couple of times on TV, on *The Best* and *Surfing the Menu*, and it's been a winner every time.

The list of ingredients seems long but it's quite easy to put together. I think it's best to use duck marylands, basically the legs. Blade mace is easy to find – it's the outside husk of the nutmeg spice. To make things easy, buy the crispy fried shallots and garlic from a good Asian store. Serves 4

6 duck legs or marylands, cut in half

1 star anise

2 sticks cassia bark or cinnamon

2 spring onions

1 stem lemongrass

4 potatoes, peeled and quartered

2 cups sunflower oil

4 dried long red chillies

1 cup Thai basil, to garnish

2 kaffir lime leaves, thinly sliced, to garnish

½ cup crispy fried shallots, to garnish

¼ cup crispy fried garlic, to garnish

Spice paste

1 tablespoon black peppercorns

½ teaspoon fennel seeds

1 teaspoon cumin seeds

1 tablespoon coriander seeds

1 blade mace

4 garlic cloves

5 long red chillies

5 French shallots

3 cm knob of galangal

2 stems lemongrass

5 coriander roots

1 cup coconut cream

100 g palm sugar

100 ml fish sauce

Position the duck legs in a large bamboo steamer. Place the star anise, cassia bark or cinnamon, spring onions and lemongrass in the steaming water. Steam for 1 hour, until the meat is tender, topping up the liquid as the duck cooks. Add the potatoes after 40 minutes.

When the duck is cooked, remove from the steamer. Reserve the steaming liquid and potatoes.

To make the spice paste, grind the peppercorns, fennel seeds, cumin seeds, coriander seeds, mace, garlic, chillies, shallots, galangal, lemongrass and coriander roots in a large mortar or blender. Grind the ingredients one at a time, in order from dry to soft, until they're all combined. Heat the coconut cream in a large frying pan over high heat, and boil until the mixture separates into an oil. Add the spice paste and fry until fragrant. Add a little steaming liquid to make a medium-thick sauce. Adjust the seasoning using the palm sugar and fish sauce. You want the curry sauce to have a sweet–salty flavour. Set aside.

Heat the sunflower oil in a wok and deep-fry the dried chillies for about 5 seconds, or until aromatic. Drain and set aside. Add the duck pieces and fry for about 5 minutes, or until crisp and golden.

Place the fried duck in the curry sauce, along with the steamed potatoes, and bring back to a boil.

Serve the duck curry garnished with the Thai basil and finely sliced lime leaves. Sprinkle over the crispy shallots and garlic and fried dried chillies.

Kingfish sashimi

Kingfish is such a wonderful fish. Rich in omega-3 and 6 (brain food), it's great simply chargrilled but raw like this it is awesome. With its natural oiliness and firm yet yielding texture, it's the perfect fish for sashimi.

This dish is a great starter to any dinner party. It also makes a wonderful canapé or *amuse-bouche*, served as small bite-sized morsels on Chinese spoons. You can buy crispy fried shallots and garlic from good Asian stores. Serves 6–8

1 x 1 kg side of kingfish, skinned, pin boned, skin and blood line removed (ask your fishmonger to do this)
2 tablespoons crispy fried shallots
2 tablespoons crispy fried garlic
½ teaspoon salt
½ teaspoon caster sugar
1 punnet coriander cress, to garnish

Dressing
3 French shallots
3 jalapeno chillies, deseeded
2½ tablespoons lime or yuzu citrus juice
2½ tablespoons shizu-infused rice vinegar
2½ tablespoons tamari
100 ml peanut oil
1 garlic clove
1 teaspoon grated ginger
salt
freshly ground black pepper

To make the dressing, place all the ingredients in a food processor and purée for 3 minutes. Strain through a fine sieve into a bowl positioned over ice and keep cold. Adjust the seasoning with a little salt and pepper if needed.

Using a sharp knife, cut slices of kingfish from the fillet. To make sure your slices are presentable, use long, single slicing movements rather than a sawing action. Arrange the slices of kingfish on a long serving platter.

Place the fried shallots and garlic, salt and caster sugar in a mortar and gently pound to coarse crumbs with a pestle.

To serve, flood the serving platter with the dressing, pouring around the slices of fish rather than over them. Garnish the fish with the coriander cress and sprinkle with the ground shallot and garlic crumbs.

Jambalaya

I cooked this recipe for a bunch of friends in Mudjimba, on Queensland's Sunshine Coast, just after New Year's Eve. A Creole version of paella, it's a great dish to impress your guests – serve it on a large dish in the centre of the table, washed down with cold beer and good wine! The key to this dish is the Cajun spice mix. Serves 6–8

2 tablespoons sunflower oil

200 g spicy chorizo sausage, thickly sliced

6–8 chicken drumsticks, skin off

250 g raw king prawns, peeled and deveined, heads and shells reserved

1 large onion, diced

1 green capsicum, diced

1 stick celery, diced

1 cup canned diced tomatoes

3 garlic cloves, chopped

6 sprigs of thyme

2 fresh bay leaves

250 g long-grain rice

3 cups chicken stock (see page 190)

1 tablespoon Cajun spice mix (see recipe opposite)

salt

freshly ground black pepper

3–4 medium male blue swimmer crabs, cooked, halved and cleaned

18–24 mussels, cleaned and debearded

6–8 oysters

2 spring onions, finely sliced, to serve

1 long green chilli, chopped, to serve

2 limes, cut into wedges, to serve

Heat the oil in a large casserole dish or electric frying pan and cook the chorizo and chicken over medium–high heat until the chicken is golden and the chorizo is crisp. Remove with a slotted spoon, leaving the oil in the pan.

Reduce the heat to low–medium. Fry the prawn heads and shells for 5 minutes, squashing them with a potato masher to extract their flavour. Remove with a slotted spoon and discard. Add the onion, capsicum and celery and sauté until soft. Stir in the tomatoes, garlic, thyme and bay leaves and cook for 5 minutes.

Add the rice, stock, chicken and chorizo to the pan, then season with the Cajun spice, salt and pepper. Bring to a simmer, cover and cook over medium heat for 10 minutes.

Fold the crab halves into the rice. Push the mussels into the rice and place the oysters on top. Cover and cook for a further 5 minutes. Turn off the heat and allow to rest for a few minutes.

Stir the rice to loosen it and serve the dish sprinkled with the spring onions, chopped chilli and lime wedges.

at home with ben

Cajun spice mix

2 cups sunflower oil
1 large onion, thinly sliced
10 garlic cloves, thinly sliced
1 tablespoon cayenne pepper
1 tablespoon smoked paprika
1 tablespoon celery salt (see page 14)
1 tablespoon dried thyme
1 teaspoon fennel seeds

Heat the oil in a wok. When hot enough to cook a piece of bread golden brown in around 10 seconds, cook the onion and garlic separately, moving them around constantly so they cook evenly. Remove them from the heat when they start to turn a light golden colour, and place them on paper towel to cool and drain. You'll notice they will continue to colour.

Place the drained and cool fried onion and garlic in a bowl, along with the remaining ingredients, and blitz to a fine powder using a hand-held blender.

The spice will keep for 1 month if stored in an airtight container.

Norfolk Christmas ham

My mum's cousin Michael Boning was a runner-up on *MasterChef UK* when Loyd Grossman was host. Michael subsequently bought a pub in Norfolk, and one year I spent a Christmas there. We cooked Christmas lunch together, including Michael's recipe for Christmas ham.

The advantage you have in England is that when you poach your pickled ham or gammon, it's so cold you can leave it in the pot outside the back door! Here in Australia I tend to work with a half leg of gammon, just so you can get it in the fridge. You may need to soak the gammon overnight prior to poaching; ask your butcher whether it needs a long soaking.

You don't have to save this one for Christmas though. It is fantastic done in the Weber with a few soaked woodchips thrown in at the last minute! Serves 8

1 x 4 kg piece gammon, on the bone
2 tablespoons brown sugar
2 tablespoons salt
handful of cloves

Marinade
2 oranges
10 whole cloves
½ cup orange juice
3 carrots, roughly chopped
2 onions, sliced
small bunch of thyme
6 juniper berries
2 sticks cinnamon
2 x 500 g jars good-quality marmalade

Soak the gammon in plenty of fresh cold water for 1 hour, or as long as the butcher tells you to.

To prepare the marinade, stab the oranges with a knife to increase the flavour, then stud each one with 5 cloves. Place the gammon in a large saucepan, along with all the marinade ingredients and enough cold water to cover. Bring to the boil, then reduce heat and simmer for 1 hour. Allow the gammon to cool completely in the liquid, leaving it overnight in a cool spot.

When ready to cook, preheat the oven to 160°C.

Take the gammon out of the marinade and place it on a baking tray. Remove the skin from the ham, leaving a layer of fat. Score lines into the fat to create diamond shapes. Cover with foil and bake for 2 hours.

Take the tray out of the oven and turn up the heat to 200°C. Combine the brown sugar and salt and rub or sprinkle all over the fat and into the cuts. Stud each diamond with a clove. Return to the oven for 30 minutes, or until the fat is golden brown and crisp.

Allow the gammon to rest for at least 30 minutes before carving.

Seafood focaccia

I have seen six blokes absolutely smash this in about two minutes! The idea is that the focaccia is the plate, absorbing the flavour and juices of the seafood. Dig in and eat the prawns, crab and mussels, then rip into the juicy and crusty bread! Serves 6

350 ml tepid water

250 g semolina flour, plus extra for dusting

15 g fresh yeast or 7 g sachet dried yeast

1 teaspoon honey

250 g Italian 00 pasta flour, plus extra for dusting

2 teaspoons salt, plus extra to season

½ bunch of basil, chopped, to garnish

2 lemons, cut into wedges, to garnish

freshly ground black pepper

Seafood topping

1 punnet cherry vine tomatoes, halved

2 green chillies, chopped

2 tablespoons chopped thyme

100 ml extra-virgin olive oil

salt

freshly ground black pepper

4 medium male blue swimmer crabs, halved and cleaned

500 g black mussels, cleaned and debearded

500 g raw king prawns, shells left on, washed

Place the warm water and semolina flour in a large bowl and combine to make a porridge. The mixture should be blood temperature. Add the yeast and honey; if using fresh yeast, use your hand to break it up into the semolina. Add the pasta flour and salt, working the dough until it is smooth, soft and not too sticky. Dust with a little flour and leave to prove at room temperature for about 45 minutes, or until the dough doubles in size.

Tip the dough out onto a clean surface. Knock back and knead the dough again. You may need to dust with a little flour to stop it from sticking. Roll out into a round, square or oval shape about 2.5 cm thick.

Dust a baking tray with semolina flour, then place the dough on top, pressing out if necessary.

Preheat the oven to 180°C.

To make the topping, combine the tomatoes, chilli, thyme and olive oil in a bowl. Season with salt and pepper and squish together with your hands to combine the flavours. Add the seafood and mix well.

Arrange the mixture on top of the focaccia, pressing the seafood into the dough. Place the bread somewhere warm to prove for roughly 20 minutes. The dough should rise and slightly envelop the seafood.

Bake the focaccia in the oven for about 20 minutes, or until bread is golden brown and seafood is cooked. Remove from the oven and garnish with the chopped basil and wedges of lemon. Season before serving.

Ceviche of Moreton Bay bug

I love the zingy, clean flavours of this dish. Ceviche is a style of Latin American cooking (or not cooking!) that is common from Peru to Mexico. It relies on the acidity of the limes to marinate and cook the flesh of the shellfish.

This recipe works just as well with lobster or crayfish. I like to plunge the shellfish into boiling water first as this makes the meat shrink away from the shell, making it easier to remove the tail meat. Serves 4

4 × 200 g Moreton Bay bugs
2 French shallots, thinly sliced
200 g cherry vine tomatoes, blanched, peeled, deseeded and halved, juice sieved and reserved
juice of 2 limes
1/3 cup olive oil
salt
freshly ground black pepper
1 avocado, halved, stoned and diced
bunch of coriander, leaves picked

Bring a large saucepan of water to the boil. Immerse the bugs in the boiling water for 30 seconds. Remove from the water and place on ice or in cold water to cool.

Remove the tail meat from the shells and dice into bite-sized pieces. Place in a bowl, along with the shallots, tomatoes and their juice, the juice of 1 lime and 2 tablespoons of olive oil. Season well with salt and pepper and marinate for anywhere from 10 minutes to 2 hours, depending on how well you like your lobster cooked. I think 20 minutes is best.

Season the avocado with the juice of 1 lime, salt, pepper and some olive oil.

To serve, position a large pastry cutter, about 6 cm in diameter, in the centre of each plate, and spoon in a quarter of the avocado. Gently combine the lobster mixture with the coriander, and divide between the rings.

Garnish each plate with a drizzle of olive oil, and remove the pastry cutters just before serving.

Fish in the bag

I used to cook this dish at the Atlantic in London. We would serve it at the table in the paper bag and the waiter would open it. One day a well-known actress from Eastenders ordered it. When the waiter went to clear the table, he asked how the meal was. She replied, 'The fish was great but I don't know about the pastry.' Just let your guests know they shouldn't eat the 'pastry'!

For even cooking, ensure your fish are the same size and shape. Serve with steamed spinach. Serves 4

50 g butter

2 leeks, halved, washed and thinly sliced

1 garlic clove, chopped

salt

freshly ground white pepper

4 × 180 g fillets goldband snapper or similar firm white-fleshed fish, skin off

2 tablespoons extra-virgin olive oil

1 telegraph cucumber, peeled and thinly sliced

juice of 1 lemon

2 tablespoons chopped dill

½ cup dry white wine

⅓ cup Japanese mayonnaise

Preheat the oven to 200°C.

Heat the butter in a saucepan, then add the leek and garlic. Gently sweat for 15 minutes, or until the leek is soft and without colour. Season with salt and pepper, then set aside and allow to cool.

Lightly season the fish with salt and pepper. Cut out four squares of baking paper – you want the sheets to be around 30 cm × 42 cm wide. Preparing one sheet at a time, brush the centre of the paper with some olive oil and place a quarter of the leek mixture on top, followed by a fillet of fish. Arrange the cucumber slices over the top of the fish fillet, positioning them closely together so they look like fish scales. Squeeze with a little lemon juice and add a pinch of dill.

Fold over two sides of paper to envelop the fish, making sure not to displace the cucumber slices. Using scissors, trim the two open edges into semicircles. Crimp the bottom edge, making firm creases to seal the parcel. Crimp most of the top edge, leaving the last corner unsealed. The parcel should resemble a pasty in shape; I like to blow air into the bag to puff it up. Pour in a little white wine, then continue crimping the last corner to completely seal the parcel. Twist the ends to secure and place the parcel on a baking tray. Complete the remaining three parcels.

Place the tray in the oven and cook for 10 minutes. The bags should puff up if you have sealed them well. Remove the tray from the oven and allow the parcels to rest for 2–3 minutes.

Combine the remaining dill, lemon juice and mayonnaise. Place the fish parcels on four plates. At the table, cut open each bag along the top crimped edge. Fold back the paper and dollop a tablespoon of the dill mayo onto each fish fillet.

leftovers

Stocks

Making homemade stock is easy. The fact that you're using leftover bones or prawn shells that have previously been cooked means you've already imparted a good deal of flavour, and it will take a little less time to make a decent stock.

Basic chicken stock

Whether you are using a chicken from the supermarket, or leftovers from cooking a Vegemite roast chicken, the advantage is that the flavour has already been created so making a tasty stock is easy.

1 leftover chicken carcass (see page 106) – bones, skin and everything
1 large carrot, diced
½ onion
1 stick celery, cut in half
5 black peppercorns
1 tomato
4 sprigs of thyme
1 flat-leaf or curly parsley stalk

Place all the ingredients in a large saucepan. Cover with cold water and bring to the boil. Simmer for 2–3 hours, then allow to stand for 30 minutes. Strain through a colander or sieve, reserving the stock.

Store the stock in the fridge if you're going to be using it in the next couple of days, or freeze until required.

You can make a soup using the strained bones and vegetables within the next day or two. Place them in a bowl and cover with plastic wrap. Allow to cool until warm, then refrigerate. When ready to make the soup, pick through the bones to collect any meat. When you heat the soup, make sure it boils for 5 minutes.

Basic prawn stock

I like to accumulate shells from maybe two prawn dinners and keep them frozen until required.

2 tablespoons vegetable oil
1 onion, diced
1 carrot, diced
1 stick celery, diced
2 tomatoes
2 garlic cloves
1 flat-leaf or curly parsley stalk
1 red chilli
leftover prawn shells and heads from about 20 prawns

Heat the oil in a large saucepan over medium heat and sweat the vegetables for 15 minutes, or until soft and the tomato has broken down into a pulp. Add the prawn shells and sweat for 5 minutes, until they turn orange. Cover with cold water and bring to the boil. Simmer for 30 minutes, then strain through a colander or sieve, reserving the stock. Allow to cool.

Store the stock in the fridge if you're going to be using it in the next couple of days, or freeze until required.

at home with ben

Pork or duck stock

Pork and duck stocks give you a more complex flavour. They are great to use when you're making Asian-inspired soups and dishes. You can also make this stock using chicken bones.

leftover bones from roast pork belly
(see page 86) or duck bones (see
pages 110–1)
5 spring onions
1 stick celery
1 star anise
1 cm piece ginger
2 garlic cloves
5 black peppercorns
1 tomato

Place all the ingredients in a large saucepan. Cover with cold water and bring to the boil. Simmer for 2 hours, then strain through a colander or sieve, reserving the stock. Allow to cool.

Store the stock in the fridge if you're going to be using it in the next couple of days, or freeze until required.

You can make a soup using the strained bones and vegetables within the next day or two. Place them in a bowl and cover with plastic wrap. Allow to cool until warm, then refrigerate. When ready to make the soup, pick through the bones to collect any meat. When you heat the soup, make sure it boils for 5 minutes.

Vegetable tom yum

This is also great with the addition of prawns, added at the same time as the mushrooms. Serves 4

1 litre chicken stock (see page 190) or
   prawn stock (see page 190)

4 yellow button squash, cut into quarters

1 stem lemongrass, peeled and chopped

3 roots coriander

1 garlic clove, peeled

2–3 red chillies, chopped

2 ripe vine tomatoes, diced

juice of 2 limes

1 tablespoon fish sauce

6 shiitake mushrooms

200 g silken tofu, cut into large cubes

4 small handfuls of bean sprouts

handful of ripped Thai basil, to garnish

Pour the stock into a large saucepan and bring to the boil. Add the squash and simmer for 10 minutes, or until tender.

Place the lemongrass, coriander, garlic and chilli in a mortar and pound with a pestle until it forms a wet paste. Add the tomatoes and gently squash with the paste. Pour in the lime juice and fish sauce. You want a blend of sour and salty, so add more lime juice or fish sauce if you need to adjust the flavours.

Add the shiitake mushrooms to the stock and cook for 1 minute, then stir in the spice paste.

Divide the tofu between four large bowls. Ladle in the soup and top each bowl with a handful of bean sprouts and garnish with the Thai basil.

Arancini

Arancini are a great way to use up leftover risotto. The tasty balls of rice are ideal as cocktail canapés, a snack or a light lunch served with salad. Serves 4

2 cups leftover risotto (see page 160)
8 bocconcini balls
4 anchovy fillets, cut in half
1 egg
1 cup milk
1 cup plain flour
3 cups panko Japanese breadcrumbs
2 cups sunflower oil
4 cups wild rocket
2½ tablespoons balsamic vinegar
2 tablespoons extra-virgin olive oil
salt
freshly ground black pepper
4 slices prosciutto (optional)
80 g parmesan, shaved, to serve

Using wet hands, shape the leftover risotto into 8 small balls, roughly similar in size. Push one bocconcini and half a fillet of anchovy into the centre of each risotto ball, then roll into a smooth, firm ball.

Combine the egg, milk and flour in a bowl and whisk into a smooth batter. Dredge each risotto ball in the batter, then remove and drain off the excess batter.

Roll each ball in the breadcrumbs, one at a time, ensuring they are well crumbed. Set aside.

Heat the sunflower oil in a small pan over medium heat. When hot enough to cook a piece of bread golden brown in around 10 seconds, carefully add two balls at a time and cook until golden brown. Remove and drain on paper towel. Repeat with the remaining balls.

Dress the rocket with the balsamic and olive oil, toss and season with salt and pepper.

Divide the salad between four plates. Place a slice of prosciutto (if using) on each plate, along with the arancini and shaved parmesan.

Roast pork and tea egg congee

Congee is a dish I first experienced as a young chef in Sydney. After work and a few drinks we would always end up in Chinatown sometime between 1 and 3 am. Congee was a popular choice when we needed nourishment, and this is my version of the preserved egg and pork congee we used to order.

Congee is basically a porridge made from either leftover rice or broken rice. It's very nutritious and is often given to the elderly or convalescing. It can be flavoured with fish, pork or chicken. This recipe uses both leftover rice and pork. Serves 4

3 cups leftover steamed rice

1 litre chicken stock (see page 190)

salt

200 g leftover roast pork belly (see page 86), thinly sliced

1 spring onion, thinly sliced

2 tablespoons crispy fried shallots

2 tablespoons crispy fried garlic

1 red chilli, chopped

soy sauce, to serve

white pepper, to serve

Tea-stained eggs

4 eggs, hardboiled

150 ml soy sauce

1 star anise

1 tablespoon gunpowder tea

To make the tea-stained eggs, roll the hardboiled eggs on the bench – hard enough to crack the shells but not so hard that they come off. Place the eggs in a small saucepan, add the soy sauce, star anise, gunpowder tea and enough water to cover. Bring to the boil, reduce heat, then simmer for 1 hour. Allow the eggs to cool in the liquid.

To make the congee, combine the leftover rice and chicken stock in a saucepan and bring to the boil. Reduce heat and simmer for 30 minutes, until the rice has broken down and the stock has thickened, then season with a little salt.

Add the sliced pork to warm in the congee, followed by the peeled and halved eggs.

Divide the congee between four bowls and garnish with the spring onion, crispy shallots and garlic and a little chopped chilli. Serve with soy sauce and white pepper.

Prawn short soup

We make this soup for my kids and they love it. Suffice to say, this is one thing my eldest boy, Herb, never complains about.

It's easy to put together if you have some chicken stock in the freezer. You can also put a little chicken meat into the filling to bulk it out, if you like. Serves 4

1 litre chicken stock (see page 190)
salt
freshly ground black pepper
¼ small iceberg lettuce, chopped
1 spring onion, chopped, to garnish
1 tablespoon finely chopped ginger, to garnish

Dumplings
500 g raw prawns, peeled and deveined
2 teaspoons fish sauce
1 spring onion, chopped
1 tablespoon sliced ginger
270 g packet wonton skins

To make the dumplings, reserve 8 prawns to garnish, then place the remainder in a blender and pulse until finely chopped. Season with fish sauce. Add the spring onion and ginger and combine.

Place 1 teaspoon of the prawn mixture in the centre of a wonton skin. Brush the outer edges of the wonton with water, then fold to form a triangle, crimping the edges together to seal.

To make the soup, bring the chicken stock to the boil in a saucepan and season to taste. Lower in the wontons and poach for about 5 minutes. Add the reserved prawns and cook for 2 minutes. Add the chopped lettuce and wilt.

To serve, divide the soup between four bowls and garnish each bowl with 2 prawns, some chopped spring onion and a little chopped ginger.

Duck and nutmeg ravioli

I used to make this dish at Monte's in London. The duck fat would be collected from slow-roasted ducks, by chilling the steaming water and skimming off the fat. Whenever you cook a duck or goose, always collect the fat as it's great for roasting potatoes. If you haven't got any leftover duck meat, you can buy it precooked at supermarkets.

I serve this dish as a starter. You could also serve it as a main, by combining the duck meat and sauce and tossing it through fresh pasta like tagliatelle. Serves 4

2 tablespoons duck fat

1 carrot, finely diced

1 large stick celery, finely diced

1 onion, finely diced

2 garlic cloves, chopped

250 g roast duck meat (see pages 110–1), picked and chopped

salt

270 g packet yellow wonton skins

1 litre duck stock (see page 191) or chicken stock (see page 190) or water

50 g parmesan, grated, to serve

1 tablespoon chopped marjoram, to garnish

Tomato sauce

2 tablespoons olive oil

1 garlic clove, chopped

400 g can diced tomatoes

½ stick cinnamon

1 red chilli, chopped

salt

freshly ground black pepper

¼ teaspoon ground nutmeg

50 g butter

Heat the duck fat in a saucepan over medium heat, then add the carrot, celery and onion. Sweat for 10 minutes, until very soft, then add the garlic and duck meat and sauté for 5 minutes. Season with salt and allow to cool.

To make the tomato sauce, heat the olive oil in a saucepan over medium heat. Sauté the garlic for 3 minutes until sticky, then add the tomatoes, cinnamon and chilli. Cook for 20 minutes to slowly reduce by half. Season with salt and pepper, and set aside.

Make the ravioli by placing a small amount of the duck meat filling in the middle of each wonton wrapper. Wet the edges with water and fold over, sealing well. Place on a tray lined with baking paper.

Bring the duck or chicken stock or water to the boil in a large saucepan. Add the ravioli and cook for 4–5 minutes, or until the wonton skins are cooked and the filling is hot. Remove to a bowl, along with ¼ cup of the cooking liquid. Cover with plastic wrap.

Heat the tomato sauce over medium heat and stir in the nutmeg and butter. When hot, add the ravioli and reserved cooking liquid and heat through.

To serve, top with the grated parmesan and chopped marjoram.

Rice paper rolls

Ripe paper rolls are one of the most instantly recognisable Vietnamese dishes. They are so easy to make. This version is a variation on the classic, and you could also use leftover roast pork, beef – anything, really! They would be awesome deep-fried.

I like making these for the kids' lunch boxes – well, Ruby's at least, as Herb would turn green if I put them in his!

Be careful with the rice paper wrappers as they are very fragile – you need to have more than you need, to allow for breakages. Buy the ones that come in the round plastic box, as it means you end up with fewer broken sheets of rice paper. Serves 4

12 rice paper wrappers
250 g chicken meat (see page 106), shredded
¼ iceberg lettuce, shredded
lime juice, to taste
fish sauce, to taste
½ bunch of mint, leaves picked and washed
½ bunch of coriander, leaves picked and washed
½ cucumber, julienned
2 tablespoons ground toasted cashews
garlic chives
sweet chilli sauce, to serve

Soak each rice paper sheet in water, one at a time, then place on a clean tea towel. Gently pat dry.

Combine the chicken and lettuce with lime juice and fish sauce to taste.

To make the rolls, place a line of mint, coriander and cucumber on the bottom edge of each rice paper wrapper, leaving the side edges clear. Top with the chicken and lettuce mixture.

Starting from the bottom edge of the wrapper, roll over once then fold in one of the side edges. Roll once more and tuck in the other edge. Sprinkle with some ground cashews and lay a single garlic chive along the length of the roll, leaving a little overhanging at one end, then completely roll. Tie with another garlic chive. Repeat this process for the remaining rice paper wrappers.

Serve the rice paper rolls with sweet chilli sauce.

Roasted pork and prawn crispy pancakes

I love these crispy pancakes! They are a great dish to share. This recipe makes two large pancakes, enough to feed four people well. You could also make several smaller pancakes, if you prefer. Serves 4

350 g rice flour

½ teaspoon ground turmeric

pinch of salt

1 teaspoon sugar

3 cups coconut milk

1 cup water

100 ml sunflower oil

8 iceberg lettuce leaves, to serve

½ bunch of mint, to serve

2 limes, cut into wedges, to serve

Filling

2 teaspoons sunflower oil

250 g leftover roast pork belly (see page 86), sliced

2 garlic cloves, chopped

1 teaspoon finely grated ginger

2 onions, sliced

large handful of bean sprouts

3 spring onions, trimmed and sliced on an angle

250 g cooked prawns, peeled and deveined

soy sauce, to taste

Make a batter by sifting the rice flour, turmeric, salt and sugar into a mixing bowl. Stir in the coconut milk, water and 1 tablespoon of sunflower oil until well combined. The batter should be smooth, with a pouring cream consistency.

To make the filling, heat the sunflower oil in a wok or large frying pan over medium heat. Add the pork and a little of the garlic and ginger and stir-fry for 2–3 minutes until hot, then set aside.

Stir-fry the onion and bean sprouts with the remaining garlic and ginger for 2 minutes. Add the spring onion, prawns and pork and season with soy sauce to taste. Set aside, keeping warm on the edge of the stove.

To make the pancakes, heat the remaining sunflower oil in a large non-stick frying pan or well-seasoned wok. Pour in enough batter to make a nice thick pancake, swirling the batter around the pan to ensure an even thickness. Cook on one side for 3–5 minutes, or until golden and crispy. When cooked, spoon some of the warm prawn and pork filling onto one half of the pancake and fold over the top.

Repeat the process with the remaining batter and filling, keeping the cooked pancakes warm under a tea towel or in the oven.

Serve with lettuce-leaf cups, mint and lime wedges. The idea is to make your own lettuce pocket filled with the pancake, mint and a squeeze of lime.

Shepherd's pie

This is a dish from my childhood. It's one of those recipes that's really about making the most of what you have on hand.

You could use raw lamb or beef mince, rather than leftover roast meat, but it would be more fatty. If you use beef you wouldn't be able to call it shepherd's pie – it would be cottage pie!

If you don't have a mincer at home, just chop the cooked meat by hand. You could also add frozen peas to the mince prior to placing it in the baking dish. Serves 4

2 tablespoons sunflower oil
1 large carrot, diced
1 large onion, diced
1 large stick celery, diced
2 garlic cloves, chopped
500 g leftover roast lamb (see page 79), minced
2 tablespoons Vegemite
¼ cup tomato sauce
2 tablespoons Worcestershire sauce
salt
freshly ground black pepper
6 potatoes, peeled and chopped
100 g butter
¼ cup milk

Heat the sunflower oil in a large saucepan over medium heat. Sauté the carrot, onion, celery and garlic for about 15 minutes, or until soft and translucent. Stir in the minced lamb and cook for about 5 minutes. Add the Vegemite, tomato and Worcestershire sauces and enough water to just cover the mixture. Simmer for about 2 hours. When cooked, season with salt and pepper, cover and leave to stand.

Preheat the oven to 180°C.

Boil the potatoes in salted water until tender. When cooked, drain and allow to steam dry. Return the potatoes to the saucepan and mash with the butter and enough milk to moisten.

Transfer the mince to a baking dish or shallow casserole dish, and cover with the mashed potatoes. Using a fork, make a hatched pattern across the top of the potatoes.

Place the dish in the oven and bake for 30 minutes, until the mashed potato is golden and the mince is hot and bubbling.

desserts

Grandma's apple pie

Apple pie is a dish that is etched into my mind, as I was raised on my grandma's baking. When my mates and I would come home from school, we would demolish the pie she had just baked in minutes. She was equally well known for her ginger cake, but that's another story.

I learnt pretty quick that the secret to a good pie is the pastry, and my gran had it nailed. I can still see her rubbing the flour and fats together by hand, with her dodgy thumb she could never straighten.

This pastry is quite short, so as soon as it's cooked you need to remove it from the oven and allow it to cool. The pastry will firm up as it cools. If you like, you could freeze any leftover pastry for another time. Serve the pie with ice-cream and custard. Serves 6

1 kg granny smith apples, peeled, cored and sliced into eighths
1 cup caster sugar, plus extra to sprinkle
juice of ½ lemon
3 whole cloves
1 star anise

Pastry
3 cups plain flour
⅓ cup custard powder
1 cup icing sugar
pinch of salt
175 g butter
175 g lard
4 egg yolks

To make the pastry, place all the ingredients except the eggs in a food processor and blend until the mixture resembles coarse breadcrumbs. Add 3 of the egg yolks and pulse until the pastry just comes together. Divide the pastry in half, and shape into two flat discs. Cover in plastic wrap and refrigerate for 2 hours.

Preheat the oven to 180°C.

Place the slices of apple in a large saucepan, along with the caster sugar, lemon juice and spices. Cook for 10–15 minutes, or until the apple slices are just tender and hold their shape.

When the pastry is ready to roll out, place each disc between two sheets of baking paper and roll to a thickness of around 3 mm.

Place one of the circles of pastry on a baking tray, leaving it on its sheet of baking paper. Pile the apple mixture in the centre of the pastry, leaving a 1 cm border around the edge. Lightly whisk the remaining egg yolk to make an egg wash, and brush along the border.

Top the apple mixture with the remaining pastry circle and press down. Use a sharp knife to trim the edge of the pastry into a neat circle, leaving a border of around 2 cm from the apple. Pinch the edges together with your thumb and forefinger.

Brush the top of the pie with the remaining egg wash and bake for 30 minutes. Remove from the oven to sprinkle with caster sugar, then return to the oven to cook for another 15 minutes, or until golden and glazed.

Banana ice-cream

There is something about banana ice-cream I just love! I'm not a big fan of raw bananas, but I could eat a box of banana Paddle Pops in one go.

Use very ripe bananas for this recipe, as firm ones tend to make the milk and cream go a bit strange. I like to serve this with Classic Chocolate Fondant (page 218). Makes 1 litre

2 cups milk
2 cups cream
200 g caster sugar
5 very ripe bananas, peeled
1 vanilla pod, split lengthways
pinch of salt
10 egg yolks
2½ tablespoons banana liqueur

Place the milk and cream in a saucepan with 100 g caster sugar, the bananas, vanilla pod and a pinch of salt. Cover with baking paper and poach for 30 minutes. Make sure the heat is low – you don't want the cream mixture to simmer.

Remove the bananas from the mixture and discard.

Combine the egg yolks, the remaining caster sugar and the banana liqueur in a heatproof bowl, and whisk together. Add half the cream mixture and whisk, then pour into the saucepan with the remaining cream mixture. Gently cook over low heat for about 15 minutes, continuing to slowly stir, until the mixture coats the back of a spoon.

Pass the custard through a sieve, then refrigerate until cold.

Churn the custard in an ice-cream machine, following the manufacturer's instructions, and freeze until required.

Bread and butter pudding

Panettone is a traditional Christmas cake from Italy, made from a butter-enriched egg and yeast dough similar to Brioche (page 24). It's absolutely perfect for making bread and butter pudding, and it means you don't have to butter the bread, as you would if you used white sliced bread. If you're not using panettone, dot 50 g sultanas and 50 g currants between the two layers of buttered bread.

When ready to serve, the pudding should be lovely and moist and ooze custard. Serve it warm with ice-cream. Serves 6

50 g butter
6 large slices panettone
8 egg yolks
175 g caster sugar
1 vanilla pod, split lengthways
300 ml milk
300 ml cream
100 g apricot jam

Preheat the oven to 160°C.

Grease a shallow, 6 cm deep baking dish with the butter. Cut the panettone slices into squares and arrange them in the baking dish in two even layers, fitting snugly side by side.

Make a custard by whisking the egg yolks and caster sugar together in a bowl until combined. Place the split vanilla pod and seeds in a saucepan with the milk and cream. Bring to a simmer, then remove the vanilla pod and pour into the egg mixture, stirring all the time.

Pour the warm custard over the panettone, pressing down so the cake absorbs the liquid. Leave the pudding to stand for 30 minutes before baking.

Place the baking dish in the oven and bake for 20 minutes, or until firm and golden. Leave to stand for 10 minutes.

While the pudding is cooking, warm the apricot jam in a small saucepan.

To serve, brush the surface of the pudding liberally with the apricot jam glaze.

Apple tarte tatin

Apples are always available, so it makes sense to use them as often as you can. This recipe works best with a firm apple like a granny smith. To make sure the apples don't stick, use an ovenproof non-stick frying pan.

Serve the tart warm with some good-quality vanilla ice-cream. Serves 6

250 g caster sugar

100 g butter

8 granny smith apples, peeled, cored and cut into quarters

plain flour, for dusting

500 g puff pastry, defrosted if frozen

2 vanilla pods, split lengthways

Make a caramel by placing the caster sugar and 2½ tablespoons of water in a clean, 24 cm non-stick frying pan. Bring to the boil, then keep boiling until the syrup starts to caramelise and turn golden brown. Remove from the heat and whisk in the butter.

Place the apple quarters in the pan and toss to coat in the caramel. Arrange the quarters so they fit snugly together, rounded-side down. Set aside.

Preheat the oven to 180°C.

Lightly flour your bench and roll the puff pastry into a shape as wide as the inside edge of your frying pan. Trim so the pastry is a vaguely round shape. Roll the pastry up around your rolling pin and lay it over the caramel and apple mixture. Tuck the edges into the frying pan to snugly encase the fruit.

Return the pan to the stovetop on medium heat and bring the caramel back to the boil.

Place the frying pan in the oven and bake the tarte tatin for about 25 minutes, or until the top is golden and crisp.

Remove from the oven and allow to rest before turning out, to avoid burning yourself with hot caramel.

While the tart is still warm, place a large plate over the frying pan. Slowly flip, so the plate is now under the pan. Gently shake to loosen the apples and lift the pan away to reveal the tarte tatin.

Rearrange any misplaced apples for presentation, and serve.

Caramel bananas

This recipe comes from the time I used to stay with my friend Tom and his family in Yorkshire. His mother knocked this sauce up for us one night, using a mixture of nuts. I think pecans are good but you can use whichever nuts you prefer.

To serve, pour the caramel bananas over vanilla ice-cream or whatever you like. Serves 4

½ cup brown sugar

½ cup pecans

50 g butter

4 ripe bananas, sliced

pinch of salt

¼ cup cream

Melt the brown sugar in a large frying pan until it starts to bubble. Add the pecans and toss to coat in the sugar. Cook until the nuts start to toast and smell lovely.

Add the butter, combine with the nuts and cook until the butter foams.

Add the slices of banana to the pan and cook until they caramelise. Season with a pinch of salt. Pour in the cream and bring to the boil. Remove from the heat and allow to cool slightly before serving.

I wasn't sure whether to put this
recipe for caramel bananas in the
breakfast or dessert chapter, as
I can easily eat them both in the
morning with pancakes and after
dinner with ice-cream.

Classic chocolate fondant

This classic French dessert is so simple. Once you've mastered it, you'll ask yourself what all the fuss is about. The key is timing. I use regular ramekins for this – they need to be the same shape and thickness, as otherwise the cooking time will be affected. You need to make an initial test fondant, to check the temperature – just make sure the temperature is the same when you cook the remaining fondants. Remember, it's all about timing!

The fondant mixture can be prepared in advance and kept in the fridge. For best results, use Valrhona or similar quality chocolate.

Serve these chocolate fondants with good-quality vanilla ice-cream, or better still, Banana Ice-cream (page 210). Serves 6

140 g unsalted butter, plus extra for buttering

100 g plain flour, plus extra for dusting

140 g dark chocolate, 70% minimum cacao

85 g caster sugar

3 eggs

3 egg yolks

cocoa or icing sugar, to serve

cream, to serve

Preheat the oven to 180°C.

Butter and flour six 140 ml ramekins.

Place the chocolate and butter in a heatproof bowl positioned over a saucepan of simmering water, making sure the bowl doesn't touch the water. Melt until thick and glossy.

Whisk the caster sugar, eggs and egg yolks together until the mixture reaches ribbon stage – thick and creamy and holding its shape.

Pour the melted chocolate over the egg mixture, and sift on the flour. Use a large metal spoon to carefully fold the flour into the mixture. Divide the mixture between the prepared ramekins, leaving space at the top for the fondants to rise a little.

To check if the temperature is right, cook a test fondant. Place one of the ramekins in the oven and bake for 9–10 minutes. When cooked, the fondant should be molten and oozy in the centre.

Place the remaining ramekins in the oven and bake for 9–10 minutes. Remove from the oven and allow to rest for a minute or two.

If the ramekins are too hot to handle, use a tea towel to turn them out onto plates. Dust the fondants with cocoa or icing sugar and serve with cream.

Lemon ricotta drizzle cake

I love the simple flavours of this cake. Buy firm, fresh ricotta from a continental deli, as you need those little chunks of creaminess to break up the texture of the cake. I like to serve this with crème fraîche. Serves 6

225 g soft butter, plus extra for buttering
250 g caster sugar
6 eggs, separated
250 g ground almonds
65 g semolina flour
juice of 3 lemons
zest of 6 lemons
300 g firm ricotta
½ cup sugar
crème fraîche, to serve

Preheat the oven to 160°C.

Grease a 25 cm springform cake tin with butter and line the base with baking paper.

Place the butter and caster sugar in a mixing machine and cream until pale. Add the egg yolks, one at a time, and combine.

Combine the ground almonds, semolina flour and half the lemon juice and zest. Fold into the butter and egg mixture.

Crumble the ricotta into the mixture and fold through.

In a separate bowl, whisk the egg whites until soft peaks form, then fold through the mixture.

Pour the cake batter into the prepared cake tin and bake in the oven for 40 minutes. Insert a skewer into the centre of the cake – if the skewer comes out clean, remove the cake from the oven and allow it to cool slightly.

To make a syrup, combine the sugar, remaining lemon juice and zest and 1 cup of water in a saucepan. Bring to the boil and reduce by half.

Serve the cake warm, with the syrup drizzled over the top and some crème fraîche on the side.

Chocolate mousse

Chocolate mousse is a winner every time! The chocolaty richness, and the sensual way it melts at the touch of your tongue. The secret is getting the volume into the mousse with your whipped egg whites.

It's important that the bowl you use to whisk the egg whites in is clean, dry and free of fat. These elements will restrict the egg whites' capacity to hold air and achieve the volume you need. To make sure that your bowl is really clean, wipe it with vinegar-moistened paper towel. Serves 6

1 teaspoon instant coffee
150 g dark chocolate, 64% minimum cacao
50 g unsalted butter
1 tablespoon runny honey
1 tablespoon Tia Maria or other coffee liqueur
3 eggs, separated
1 cup cream
sprigs of mint, to garnish
strawberries, to garnish

Dissolve the instant coffee in 2 teaspoons of hot water. Place the chocolate, butter, honey and dissolved coffee in a heatproof bowl positioned over a saucepan of barely simmering water, making sure the bowl doesn't touch the water. Stir until the chocolate is melted.

Remove the bowl from the heat and stir in the Tia Maria and egg yolks. Allow to cool – when you dab some of the mixture on your lips, it should feel warm.

Use electric beaters to whisk the egg whites in a clean, dry bowl for 3–5 minutes, until foamy and soft peaks form. In a separate bowl, whip the cream to soft peaks, then keep chilled.

When the chocolate is cool, gently fold in a third of the chilled whipped cream. Gently fold in half the whisked egg white, keeping as much air in the mixture as possible. Fold in the remaining egg white, followed by the remaining cream.

Divide the mousse among six 1-cup serving glasses, or a large bowl, and chill for 4–6 hours to set.

Serve garnished with sprigs of mint and strawberries.

Golden syrup pudding

This is another childhood recipe that has stayed with me. I have lightened it up with the addition of breadcrumbs, ground almonds and, of course, rum.

To keep things easy, serve the pudding with the warmed golden syrup and some bought custard. Serves 6

125 g caster sugar
225 g soft butter
2 eggs
100 g self-raising flour
1 vanilla pod, split lengthways
50 g breadcrumbs
25 g ground almonds
100 ml tepid milk
2½ tablespoons rum
1½ cups golden syrup

To make the batter, cream the caster sugar and 125 g of butter in a mixing machine until pale. Add the eggs, one at a time, and combine. Add the flour, vanilla seeds, breadcrumbs and ground almonds and mix until combined. Pour in enough warm milk to reach a dropping consistency.

Grease a 1 litre pudding basin well with the remaining butter. Place the vanilla pod in the basin. Combine the rum and 1 cup of golden syrup, then pour over the vanilla pod.

Pour the batter over the syrup, spreading evenly. Cover the top of the pudding basin with baking paper and secure with butchers twine.

Place a small saucer in the base of a large heavy-bottomed saucepan and half fill the pan with boiling water. Place the pudding basin on top of the saucer; the water should come halfway up the side. Cover the saucepan with a lid and simmer for 1 hour. Check the liquid level from time to time to ensure there is enough water.

To check if the pudding is cooked, pierce it with a skewer – if the skewer comes out clean, the pudding is ready.

When cooked, remove the pudding from the saucepan and allow to rest for 5 minutes before turning out onto a large serving plate.

Warm the remaining golden syrup and serve with the pudding.

It's important your kids engage with food. They might make a mess, but they will have loads of fun. The hardest part of cooking with my kids is getting them all on one chair, as they all want to do the stirring!

Roly poly

My earliest memories of growing up in England are my grandma's cooking and being in trouble, both in equal measure. Grandma's cooking was all about good, honest Norfolk fare – dumplings, apple pies, treacle tart and, best of all, roly poly! At the age of five, it's something you swear you could eat three times a day, every day of your life! Of course, if you did you'd soon end up a roly poly yourself, such is the calorific impact of this, the crown prince of sweet, stodgy English puddings. Ideally, you need to use lard. You don't have to use an animal lard, vegetable suet will do, and at a pinch you could use a good-quality unsalted butter.

Serves 6

375 g plain flour
3 teaspoons baking powder
100 g caster sugar, plus extra to sprinkle
180 g lard
zest of 1½ lemons
150 ml milk
2 tablespoons raspberry jam
¼ punnet blackberries
¼ punnet raspberries
cream and fresh berries, to serve

Combine the flour, baking powder and caster sugar in a large bowl. Using your fingertips, rub in the lard until you get a fine crumb texture. Add the lemon zest, stir in the milk and knead the mixture into a dough. On a floured sheet of baking paper, roll out into a square about 1 cm thick. Spread the dough evenly with the jam, top with the berries and sprinkle with a little caster sugar.

Carefully roll the roly poly into a log shape, making sure you have an equal distribution of fruit.

Tear off a sheet of baking paper, making sure it is wide enough and long enough to wrap around the roly poly. Fold a 2.5 cm pleat in the middle of the sheet of paper, to allow for the pudding to expand.

Carefully place the roly poly directly on top of the crease. Fold over the sides of paper to envelop the pudding and tie each end firmly with butchers twine. Secure the middle with a slightly looser piece of twine.

Place a wire rack in a baking tin and pour in enough hot water to fill to just below the rack. Place the roly poly on the rack and cover the tin with foil.

Place the tin in the oven and steam for 30 minutes. To check if the pudding is cooked, insert a skewer – if the skewer comes out clean, the roly poly is ready. Allow to rest for 10 minutes.

Carefully unwrap the roly poly and sprinkle liberally with caster sugar. Cut into slices and serve with cream and fresh berries.

Foolproof soufflé

This is a great recipe because you can make the soufflés in advance, put them in the fridge for a few hours and cook them when you need them.

As for Classic Chocolate Fondant (page 218), you will need to do a test run to check that the temperature is right.

Make sure you don't over whisk and break the egg whites, as the mix won't hold the air required to lift the soufflés. It's also a great idea to freeze egg whites, as defrosted egg white works really well for whisking. Serves 6

2 cups milk
2 vanilla pods, split lengthways
½ cup cornflour
250 g dark chocolate, 64% minimum cacao, roughly chopped
5 egg yolks
250 g soft butter
100 g dark chocolate, 70% minimum cacao, grated, to dust
2 tablespoons cocoa powder, to dust
10 egg whites
pinch of salt
100 g caster sugar
1 punnet raspberries
cocoa or icing sugar, to serve

To make the chocolate soufflé base, place the milk and vanilla pods in a saucepan and bring to the boil. Combine the cornflour with 100 ml of water. When the milk comes to the boil, whisk in the cornflour, a little at a time to avoid lumps. Allow the mixture to come to the boil again, then cook, while whisking, for about 3 minutes. Remove from the heat and whisk in the chocolate, then the egg yolks. Set aside to cool.

Preheat the oven to 175°C.

Grease six 200 ml ovenproof moulds by brushing the bases liberally with the soft butter. Brush the sides, using upward strokes to help the soufflé rise. Dust the moulds with grated chocolate and cocoa powder.

Place the egg whites in a very clean, dry mixing machine, along with the salt. Start whisking at high speed, gradually adding the caster sugar, a little at a time, until the egg whites start to thicken and form stiff peaks.

Measure 600 g of the chocolate soufflé base into a large bowl and whisk until smooth. Mix in a little of the whisked egg whites to loosen the mixture, then slowly and gently cut in the remaining egg whites.

Place some fresh raspberries in the bottom of the prepared moulds, reserving some to serve. Using a palette knife, fill each mould evenly with the soufflé mixture. Begin by scraping in the mixture at the edges, at a 45-degree angle. Fill the middle, then flatten the top off nice and smoothly. If you don't fill the moulds

evenly, they won't rise evenly. Make sure there's no overspill, as this will stick to the mould and prevent the soufflé from rising. Clean any mixture off the inside lip of the moulds.

To check if the temperature is right, cook a test soufflé. Place one of the soufflés in the oven and cook for 14 minutes. If the temperature is right, place the remaining soufflés in the oven to cook for 14 minutes.

To serve, dust the soufflés with cocoa or icing sugar and dot with the reserved raspberries.

As Billy Shakespeare once said, ''Tis an ill cook that cannot lick his own fingers.' So get your hands dirty when you're in the kitchen. Feel it, taste it, cook it!

'Soufflés are so yum.'

chef's

Most of the ingredients in this book can be bought from general supermarkets or specialty stores. I always try to buy the best ingredients I can afford, which doesn't mean that everything always has to be organic or that meat needs to be sourced from rare breeds reared by monks in virgin forests! But if it's possible for me to buy the best, I will.

Asafoetida This powder is used widely in Indian cooking and can be found at most Asian stores and some supermarkets. It has quite a pungent flavour when raw, but becomes milder once it is cooked.

Chipotles Chipotles are smoked jalapeno chillies and can be found at good European delis. Look for ones in adobo sauce, which is a spicy tomato sauce.

Cream Cream is always pure cream with a fat content of 35%, unless stated otherwise.

Crispy fried shallots and garlic I like to use Cock brand.

Dried anchovies These can be found in Chinese supermarkets. Look for the smallest fish, and ones that are not broken.

Eggs Eggs are standard medium 55 g, and should be free-range wherever possible.

Fish sauce I like to use Mega Chef brand.

Garlic and ginger paste Garlic and ginger paste is made by simply puréeing garlic or ginger in a food processor with a little sunflower oil to loosen to a smooth consistency.

Golden syrup I like to use Lyle's golden syrup.

notes

Harissa Harissa is a hot chilli paste. The best harissa pastes are the ones with the simplest ingredients. I generally avoid buying harissa in a tube.

Herbs I generally use fresh herbs. If you have leftover fresh herbs, try drying them in a very low oven and then storing them in an airtight container.

Meat Try to buy the best quality Australian meat you can afford. When buying pork, ask your butcher about the breed of the animal, as this is quite important. Black Berkshire pigs are a rare breed and are especially flavoursome. When it comes to kangaroo, I generally buy loins. Just be aware that they vary greatly in size.

Oils I generally use sunflower oil for frying, and sunflower or peanut oil for Asian dressings.

Oyster sauce I like to use Mega Chef brand.

Poultry Try to buy free-range poultry whenever you can. Organic is also good, but can be a bit more expensive.

Salt Use a good-quality salt for seasoning and cheaper salt to add to water when blanching or boiling. Murray River salt is a good Aussie salt.

Seafood Check out the Australian Marine Conservation Society's website (www.amcs.org.au) to find out which species are the most sustainable.

Shizu Shizu is a Japanese cress also known as parilla.

index

at home with ben

thanks

Ever tried writing a cookbook and opening a restaurant at the same time? My advice is don't try it!

It requires extreme patience from both the people around you and those directly involved! So for this I owe my heartfelt thanks to all those at Hardie Grant – Julie Pinkham, Fran Berry, Paul McNally, Jane Winning, Bernie Gill (who deals with my endless phone calls), Keiran Rogers (who I hope to have a cast with someday), Roxy Ryan and the rest of the team.

Thank you to the guys who worked closely on the book – Jean Kingett for editing my recipes so well, Gayna Murphy for her great design and for getting my vibe, Mark Roper for his fantastic work behind the lens and Georgia Young for her beautiful styling. Thanks to Pete, Victor and Karina for all of their hard work during the photo shoot.

Thanks also to the many people who have inspired me with their home cooking, generosity and hospitality!

To my new team at the South Bank Surf Club and to Sydney Stranger, my head chef, for being a star!

To my brand sponsors – Penfolds, Barbeques Galore, Wiltshire and Australian Fine China – for their faith and support. To Daniel and Holly Feller at Talisman for their support and belief in what we can achieve!

To Ursula Nairn and Mandy Biffin for their huge efforts when testing my recipes!

And last but by far not least, thank you to my beautiful family – Dee, Ruby, Herb and Cash – without whom my life would be empty! Thank you for your extreme patience and for picking up the work load when I am focused elsewhere. This book is for you!

And to anyone who I have missed, sorry but you're in my heart!

love Ben

Published in 2010 by Hardie Grant Books

Hardie Grant Books (Australia)
85 High Street
Prahran, Victoria 3181
www.hardiegrant.com.au

Hardie Grant Books (UK)
Second Floor, North Suite
Dudley House
Southampton Street
London WC2E 7HF
www.hardiegrant.co.uk

Cataloguing-in-Publication data is available from the
National Library of Australia.

ISBN: 978 1 74066 870 5

Design by Gayna Murphy, Greendot Design
Photography by Mark Roper
Edited by Jean Kingett
Styling by Georgia Young
Colour reproduction by Splitting Image Colour Studio
Printed and bound in China by C & C Offset Printing

10 9 8 7 6 5 4 3 2 1

The publisher would like to thank the following for their
generosity in supplying props for the book: Market Imports,
Safari Living, Made in Japan, House of Orange, 4M, Angelucci,
North Carlton Ceramics and Altamira.